Peacemaker's A,B,Cs for Young Children

A Guide for Teaching Conflict Resolution With A Peace Table

Contents

GCFP Goals

To empower parents, teachers, and older children
to use their peacemaking skills and become
role models and mentors of peace for young
children.

To increase adults' and children's abilities to
employ conflict resolution skills at home,
school, and in communities.

To enhance adults' and children's abilities to
interact compassionately and empathically
with the world's diverse people.

To enhance adults' and children's awareness of the
interconnectedness and interdependence of all
life.

To help children understand themselves and their
society through the study of great peacemakers.

To help adults and children become aware of their
personal opportunities for justice, service, and
social action.

To guide teachers in developing an integrated
curriculum for developing the peacemaking
skills of students.

GCFP Services

Publishes a quarterly newsletter: *Peacemaker's
News*™.

Designs and manufactures hands-on learning
materials for children and adults, to help them
develop skills for peacemaking.

Provides *Peacemaker*ˢᴹ character visits and
concerts for schools, preschools, and events.

Provides teacher in-services and classroom visits
for early childhood through grade 6 teachers,
trains trainers, and facilitates workshops for
community and business.

Provides anti-bias and conflict resolution education for parents and families.

Researches current peace literature and networks
with other organizations to continue to provide
the most current information in the peace
education field.

**Growing Communities for Peace™
is a nonprofit organization,
serving communities nationwide.**

About the Authors

Rebecca Janke, M.Ed. is a peace education consultant and writer, and
co-founder and co-director of Growing Communities for Peace™. She
has 20 years of teaching experi-
ence, twelve of which were spent
teaching at and administrating her
own school. This school operated
a peace camp for several summers, and ultimately worked
toward infusing the entire curriculum with peacemaking skills
development and resources.

Rebecca Janke

Rebecca brings a wide range of
educational perspectives to this
work, along with compassion for
the needs of teachers, children and
parents. A large part of her work is inventing and developing practical
applications to make comprehensive peacemaking knowledge accessible
to young children.

She is the author of an annotated bibliography *The Teacher's Annotated Guide to Peacemaking Resources*, and numerous articles on
peacemaking. She co-creates *Peacemaker*™ hands-on learning
products, and is co-creator of the *Peacemaker*™ character.

Rebecca received her Master's Degree in Education from Xavier
University.   She is a certified Pre-K through 6th grade teacher, and has
given numerous peace education seminars, workshops, and retreats for
parents, and for teachers.

**Julie Penshorn Peterson,
MBC** is co-founder and co-
director of Growing Communities for Peace™ and co-
creator of the *Peacemaker*ˢᴹ
character and *Peacemaker
Products*™. As
*Peacemaker*ˢᴹ Julie performs
for groups all over the country
on autoharp, banjo and guitar.
She also facilitates trainings.
Julie's Master's Degree is in
Business Communications.

Julie P. Peterson, as
*Peacemaker*ˢᴹ

A musician, writer, and a
concerned parent, Julie writes
and performs skill-building songs on the topics of peacemaking, care
of the planet, and love for self and others. She is the primary singer
and songwriter of *Peacemaker's*ˢᴹ music. Recently she completed the
recording *We Can Solve it Peacefully* (available through Growing
Communities for Peace™) which includes 14 songs and dialogs and
helps children learn peacemaking skills.

Implementation Suggestions

This book was written with the intent of providing a framework for early childhood teachers, K-3 elementary teachers, family child care providers, and those teaching in spiritual traditions, to create communities of peacemakers. Readers will be able to improve their skills to design a peacemaking environment, be more effective peaceful role models for children, and help children learn peacemaking skills.

Although peace education covers a wide variety of subjects, this book focuses on informal and formal conflict resolution with young children, all designed to help children develop skills to get along with others. The more capable we are at this, the more apt we are to enter into the other components of peace education. (Please see Chapter II for other components.)

Once you invest the time into implementing peacemaking skill lessons, the return on your investment will be more time for teaching, because children eventually are able to prevent and/or resolve their conflicts with little or no teacher intervention.

Beginning these lessons on your first day together with a new group of children is ideal. Continue with the lessons in sequential order, at your own pace, until all the material has been covered. We suggest presenting at least one lesson a day. You can choose additional exercises, games and activities from the **Extensions and Variations** sections of the lesson to support your teaching. When three-year-olds are with four- and five-year-olds, they learn these skills more easily due to the modeling of their peers. If you teach a class with only three-year-olds, you may want to use a portion of a lesson at one time and/or adapt it. For children who are reading, several reading and writing exercises are suggested. There is no need to hurry to complete an entire lesson each time. The process is just as important as the outcome. You and the children will feel more peaceful when you work at a pace that's respectful to you and your particular setting.

This book is designed for ease of use. Specific skill-building lessons are included for teachers who prefer step-by-step guidance. If you prefer to be more spontaneous, the lessons will help you clearly understand and convey the essential concepts in your own style. The first two chapters help the reader design a more peaceful physical and emotional environment so children are encouraged to see and experience peace. Chapters III and IV include several suggested lessons to enhance the classroom community and help the children learn conflict resolution skills.

When you "twinkle" with excitement, the children will take a keen interest. These presentations depend on your enthusiasm!

If you are part of a K-6 elementary program, we suggest training the 4th, 5th and 6th graders as peacemaking mentors. These older students can receive training and then lend their support to this peace process, on the playground, in hallways, in lunchrooms and on busses. This approach empowers your entire school to be a community of peacemakers!

We hope you will use your creative energies to add to this work!

We created the *Peacemaker*^{SM} character as a mentor, to inspire children to reach their highest potential as peacemakers. The character helps them call themselves peacemakers, and become interested in beginning a conscious study of what that means. We are convinced that if young children learn to celebrate the peacemaker in each person, and learn that peacemaking is possible for *them*, they will find opportunities throughout their lives to bring more peace into the world.

Several *Peacemaker Products*^{TM} are mentioned in this book. The products were developed by the authors to bring a (previously lacking) hands-on learning approach to the field of conflict resolution. Our products include: *Peacemaker's*^{SM} audiotape, *We Can Solve it Peacefully,* the *Peacemaker Puppet*^{TM}, *Peacemaker's A,B,Cs of Conflict Resolution*^{TM} chart, and *Peacemaker's Conflict Resolution Cubes*^{TM}. Each one has been lovingly designed and prepared with efficacy, ease of use, cost, and environmental impact considered.

The tape is important because it is effective with auditory learners. The lyrics are included in this book, but they do not compare with the music, which provides the key concepts in a fun and infectious way (the tape may be available at your library).

Teachers using this book without a *Peacemaker Puppet*^{TM} may enlarge and copy the drawing of the *Peacemaker*^{SM} character, attach it to a flat stick, and us it as a paper puppet. The cloth puppet is much more durable and can be put in the drama area for children to act out peace stories and plays. Please see the enclosed flyer with detailed descriptions of these learning tools.

Violence, Peace, Peacemaking, and Peace Education:
Some Definitions

Physical violence

is damage done through words or actions to people, animals, or the Earth.

Structural violence

is damage done to the potential for human fulfillment by structures or institutions which unevenly distribute resources and power over those resources as in the cases of economic, political or social discrimination, manipulation or oppression.[1]

Violence

1. is a learned behavior;
2. is reinforced by our society;
3. can be passed on from generation to generation (through role modeling and other means);
4. can be unlearned (there are alternatives);
5. implies a lack of responsibility for one's behavior;
6. is not justified by provocation.[2]

Peace

1. is more than vague, sentimental impressions;
2. is more than the opposite of war, or the aftermath of war; it must be accompanied by social and economic justice;
3. depends upon the lack of both physical and structural violence;
4. is a positive, dynamic effort toward the transformation of relationships at all levels of human interaction: personal, interpersonal, community, national and international;
5. is possible;
6. is an active way of life, constantly being built through the creative resolution of conflict and the building of trusting relationships;
7. does not exclude conflicts. It implies a willingness and competence to approach conflict nonviolently and creatively;
8. requires changes in both attitudes and conditions (For example, it must be accompanied by changes in perceptions regarding power and changes in the production and distribution of resources within and between societies.);
9. is the result of constant work (It may take time and may be difficult to achieve).[3]

Peacemaking

1. is action-oriented;
2. requires specific skills in, and attitudes toward human relations and organizational behavior;
3. can be learned;
4. negates the use of violence;
5. may occur at different stages of a conflict;
6. is not the smoothing over of differences. It regains respect for all;
7. contributes to the fulfillment of basic human rights and values -- such as economic well-being, social justice, and cultural participation;
8. promotes more just, less exploitative, social, economic and political systems.[3]

Peace Education

1. draws out from people their desires to live in peace;
2. provides awareness of alternatives to violence;
3. consists of teaching skills, content, and a peaceful pedagogy;
4. examines the roots and causes of violence;
5. empowers students to confront their fears of violence;
6. helps build a peaceful culture to counteract militarism;
7. challenges violent ways of thinking and acting;
8. promotes loving behavior towards oneself, others, and the environment.[4]

Resources:

[1] Adapted from Johan Galtung, "Violence, Peace and Peace Research," *Journal of Peace Research*, No. 3, 1969, pp. 167-191.

[2] Adapted from a lecture by Dave Mathews of Wilder Foundation, St. Paul, Minn., May 6th, 1994, at Humphrey Institute, Mpls., Minnesota.

[3] Adapted from Susan Carpenter, *A Repertoire of Peacemaking Skills* (Consortium on Peace Research, Education and Development, 1977).

[4] Adapted from Ian M. Harris, *Peace Education* (McFarland and Co., Jefferson, NC, 1988.)

Additional Reading:

G. Abrams & F. Schmidt, *Peace is In Our Hands* (1974). Can be borrowed from Jane Adams Peace Assn., 1213 Race St., Phila., PA 19107

M. Montessori, Peace and Education, Theosophical Pub., Adyar Madras, 600 020, India

CHAPTER I
Overview of Peace Education

Violence in the United States is rampant. In 1991, 38,317 people in the United States died from firearm-related injuries.[1] In 1992, 37% of the childhood deaths were due to physical neglect and 58% as a result of physical abuse.[2] In the United States, 3.3 million children between ages 3 and 17 years, are yearly at risk of exposure to parental violence.[3]

"The strongest developmental predictor of a child's involvement in violence is a history of previous violence . . . because aggressive habits learned early in life are the foundation for later behavior. Social and cultural influences in early childhood may have a lifelong impact on a child's attitudes toward violence and likelihood of involvement with violence."[4]

Both Dr. Martin Luther King Jr. and Mahatma Gandhi believed nonviolence is the most powerful force we humans possess, but we neglect to educate our children about it. Rather, we fill their heads with violent images and model violent ways to resolve conflicts.

The hope for our shared future lies with concerned individuals who do not accept the rising tide of violence as inevitable; who understand the power of nonviolence, and are committed to role modeling, educating, and trying to building a peaceful world.

A child's environment and skill development is critical to the ability to make nonviolent choices each day. Each developmental stage of human life offers unique educational opportunities. When children have a history of resolving conflicts effectively and nonviolently, they are less fearful or skeptical of the process, and are more apt to engage in it again, thus continuing their skill development.

There are many complex underlying causes of violence, including prejudice, injustice and poverty. Because all people suffering from these conditions do not become violent, violent behavior must be **directly related to choices people make** based on their:
1) level of skills for employing alternatives to violence and conflict resolution;
2) attitude toward themselves and others.
3) commitment to nonviolence

Low self esteem and lack of respect for others can lead to an attitude of separation and/or attempted domination over other people, as well as provide a conviction that conflict is an opportunity to prove one's power. However, children can understand the need to develop a *conflict partnership,* a term coined by Dudley Weeks.[5] This attitude empowers people to work *together* to solve problems and helps them preserve their relationship; it moves the dialog away from "me" versus "you" and toward a more collaborative approach where *we* have a problem to work out together, and *we* need each other's perspective to have enough information to find an agreeable solution.

Nonviolent conflict resolution skills cannot be internalized by children when they do not find them relevant, or believe in their efficacy. **The peace table process won't be as effective if taught in isolation, without first developing accompanying values.** We believe, in order to build a solid foundation for emerging peacemakers, it is necessary to begin with implicit peace education (the lower segment of the above pyramid) and move to explicit peace education (the second segment). When children have the skills and the culture provided by the lower two segments, they

The Peacemaker[SM] *Pyramid*

Empowerment: Service and Social action as peacemakers

Explicit peace education: Alternatives to violence. Peace table process. Mediation. Active listening. Creative problem solving. Consensus decision-making

Implicit peace education: Community building. Infusing the curriculum. Power of love. Personal responsibility. Cooling off. Guidelines. Adult role modeling. Design of environment. Cooperation. Fairness. Sharing. Interrelatedness of all.

are then empowered to reach their maximum potential as peacemakers -- the third segment.

Implicit peace education is that part of peacemaking necessary to build and support a peacemaking community. It includes the design of the environment for peace, peaceful work patterns, infusing peace into all aspects of the curriculum, peaceful role modeling of adults, developing compassionate communication skills, and accepting personal responsibility for one's feelings and actions.

Explicit peace education includes recognizing and practicing alternatives to violence, and developing skills for resolving conflicts nonviolently.

Empowerment as peacemakers includes becoming involved in service and nonviolent social action to promote a more just and peaceful world. It involves the ability to make a difference beyond the classroom community, as local, national and global peacemaking citizens, respecting justice, caring for the earth, and creating and maintaining peaceful families and communities.

Peacemaker^SM and children practicing conflict resolution at a peace table

The pyramid has four sides, symbolic of four levels of social organization:
1. the family;
2. the local community/school/spiritual traditions;
3. society at large, in the national arena
4. the international community

On every side, peacemaking skills must be nurtured, for optimum reduction in physical and structural violence. This must be accompanied by implicit and explicit peace education leading to empowerment as a peacemaker.

For many children there are weaknesses that threaten the structural integrity of their pyramid. One or more of the sides may not be solid:
1. Families may not provide an environment in which peacemaking skills can thrive, and they may lack the knowledge to model or teach nonviolent conflict resolution skills. Many of us did not learn these skills as children, and have ineffective conflict resolution styles which we role model for our children. Some families face economic hardship, and/or have too many responsibilities that overwhelm them. There may be alcohol, drugs or verbal or physical abuse involved.

2. On another side of the pyramid, local communities may not demonstrate healthy norms or provide a positive school climate respecting the needs of all students. Negative peer influence and lack of job opportunities also are important factors. Communities may not provide adequate support to families, encourage parental involvement with their children's education, or provide enough extra-curricular or safe evening activities. Focusing on punishment rather than providing alternatives to violence or other empowering educational opportunities, as well as community leaders such as police, role modeling violent behavior, are additional challenges.

3. On the national side, the media's focus on the negative and the plethora of violent images, set violence as the standard. The widespread lack of confidence in the political process and the uninspiring role modeling of national "leaders," leads to apathy and hopelessness. Focusing on our differences rather than our commonalities, leads to prejudiced behaviors.

4. On the international side, we exploit each other, looking at the short-term bottom line (rather than the

long-term) as the determinant of our behavior, and ignore the health of the environment. Children are often the innocent victims of the resulting international disputes, since we see war and policies of separation as options for resolving our conflicts.

All of us have a critical role in demonstrating and valuing peacemaking skills, and in participating in a direct and helpful way in the lives of children we know.[6]

As the saying goes, "It takes a whole village to raise a child." Grandparents, church members, work groups, friends and neighbors can act to develop a community spirit drawing them *toward* others rather than pushing them *away*. Much like one drop of water joined with others overcomes even the most resistant stone with its persistent flow, so the synergy created by the commitment to the common "we," is capable of overcoming a great deal of the loneliness and isolation leading to violent, selfish acts for the benefit of "me."

Children learn to care for others and to distinguish right from wrong by internalizing the care they receive, and applying it in relationships with others. If this process is short-circuited, via emotional and/or environmental chaos, abuse, or neglect, children have much greater difficulty developing nonviolent habits. Community norms that support nonviolent and respectful behavior have been demonstrated to make a positive difference in the lives of youth.[7] The community can demonstrate and model the love and understanding the child needs to learn. Thus, the role of the *village*, in helping the child develop empathy and compassion, becomes key to ensuring that every child receives the necessary support and love, *no matter what his or her circumstances in life may be.*

One critical link between families and communities is child care providers and teachers, who have become the primary extended family of many of our children. They are a major factor in the health of the next generation through their ability to educate parents and bond with children. Resiliency research shows, that abused children who are able to surmount their difficulties, are impacted by the presence of a loving, consistent, trusted individual in their lives. A teacher can be that person. He or she also can be an important link for whole families' education in child development and peacemaking skills.

As we begin to understand the essential role our

commitment to peacemaking has in our lives, and the lives of those we teach, we will continually find ourselves looking for ways to infuse our educational subjects with peace curriculum. **Infusing the curriculum** means providing peace education in all subjects and throughout the routine of the day. The curriculum will become more alive because the children can see how their learning relates to becoming more skilled as peacemakers, and each subject area will provide opportunities for exploring peace from a new perspective. Our own creativity, our mentors, and our resources will help us continually discover new ways to integrate educational goals with peacemaking goals.[8]

Since 80% of our personality and world view is established by age eight, we believe it is imperative that peacemaking and conflict resolution skills be viewed as essential components of excellent education, and be taught to all children. As Gandhi said, "If we are to have real peace in this world, we shall have to begin with the children." When we act to develop the structural integrity of each child's *Peacemaker Pyramid* supported on *all sides,* at every level, we take a positive step toward peace.

References:
[1] *Minnesota Monthly: A Special Report*, The Minnesota Action Plan to End Gun Violence, (St. Paul, MM, Feb., 1995).
[2] National Committee for Prevention of Child Abuse, 1993.
[3] P. Jaffe, D. Wolfe & S. Kaye Wilson, *Children of Battered Women,* (National Committee for Prev. of Child Abuse: 1990).
[4] N. Biele, *Violence Prevention: 1994 Report to the Minnesota State Legislature,* (Saint Paul: Office of Drug Policy and Violence Prevention, 1994).
[5] D. Weeks, *Eight Essential Steps to Conflict Resolution,* (New York: G.P Putnam, 1992).
[6] The Carnegie Corporation of New York, *Starting Points: Meeting the Needs of Our Youngest Children,* (NY: Carnegie, 1994).
[7] J.D. Hawkins & R.F. Catalano, *Communities That Care.* (Seattle, WA, 1991).
[8] See R. Janke, *The Teachers Annotated Guide to Peacemaking Resources* (in press) Growing Communities for Peace™.

Additional Reading
B. Reardon (1988). *Comprehensive Peace Education: Educating for Global Responsibility,* Teachers College Press, Teachers College, Columbia University, NY.
The Child Development Project, *At Home in Our Schools: A Guide to Schoolwide Activities that Build Community* (1994). Available through ASCD, 1250 N. Pitt St., Alexandria, VA 22314 (Grades K-6).
I. M. Harris (1988). *Peace Education*, MacFarland and Co., Jefferson, NC.

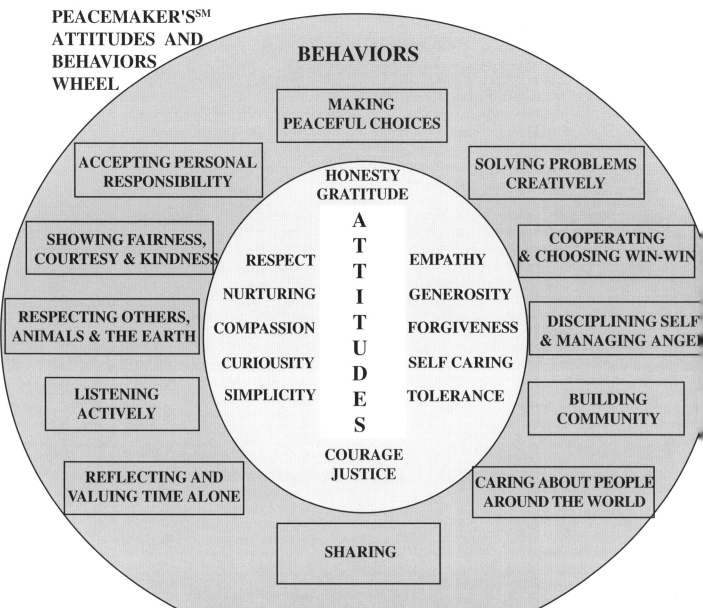

PEACEMAKER'S[SM] **ATTITUDES AND BEHAVIORS WHEEL**

BEHAVIORS

MAKING PEACEFUL CHOICES

ACCEPTING PERSONAL RESPONSIBILITY

SOLVING PROBLEMS CREATIVELY

SHOWING FAIRNESS, COURTESY & KINDNESS

COOPERATING & CHOOSING WIN-WIN

RESPECTING OTHERS, ANIMALS & THE EARTH

DISCIPLINING SELF & MANAGING ANGER

LISTENING ACTIVELY

BUILDING COMMUNITY

REFLECTING AND VALUING TIME ALONE

CARING ABOUT PEOPLE AROUND THE WORLD

SHARING

HONESTY GRATITUDE

ATTITUDES

RESPECT EMPATHY
NURTURING GENEROSITY
COMPASSION FORGIVENESS
CURIOUSITY SELF CARING
SIMPLICITY TOLERANCE

COURAGE JUSTICE

Children embrace **attitudes** and values (as shown in the inner circle), as they develop skills. Those attitudes, values and skills are manifested in their **behaviors** (as in the outer circle).

The process of developing peaceful attitudes and behaviors is ongoing. While children have great ability to develop the attitudes and values listed in the inner circle, these attitudes need reinforcement through skill-building opportunities. It is important to address children's needs from the inside circle out, **and** from the outside in.

The attitudes or values of peacemaking will best be assimilated by the children through interacting with role models who are demonstrating them, in a peaceful environment (inner circle). At the same time, skill-building exercises and lessons will develop positive attitudes and values (outer circle) that peace educators hope to help children internalize.

Both implicit and explicit peace education are necessary for peace and peacemaking to become the standard.

Additional Reading

H. Huffman (1994) *Developing A Character Education Program: One District's Experience*, ASCD, Alexandria, VA.

W. J. Bennet, *The Book of Virtues*, Health Communications, Inc., 3201 SW 15th St. Deerfield Beach, FL 33442-8190.

J. Benninga, *Moral, Character and Civic Education in the Elementary School*, Teachers College Press, Teachers College, Columbia University, New York, NY 10027.

S. S. Riley, *How to Generate Values in Young Children: Integrity, Honesty, Individuality, Self-confidence and Wisdom*, NAEYC, Washington, DC.

CHAPTER II
THE BASE OF THE PYRAMID: MAKING A PLACE FOR PEACE

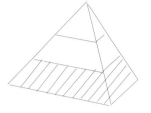

Teachers of young children are at the beginning of the wonderful lifelong enterprise of nurturing a human spirit. What we do, as teachers, contributes to the man or woman the child becomes, for it is in the early years the personality is formed.

We need to reach out to the children's hearts as well as their minds. We do this by creating a place of safety where children are free to investigate the world around them, to appreciate their shared humanity, and to discover their inner landscape of nonviolence and compassion.

In *Peace Is Every Step,* Thich Nhat Hanh writes, "Peace is all around us; that is not the question. What is in question is our ability to see it."[1] And since, as Ernie Larson, says, "What we see, we practice, and what we practice, we become,"[2] it's essential to increase our ability to "see peace."

Resources:
[1] T. N. Hanh, *Peace is Every Step* (1991). Parallax Press, PO Box 7355, Berkeley, CA 94707.
[2] E. Larson, Adapted from speech, Mpls., MN May 5, 1993.

Peacemaker's Checklist for Creating a Peaceful Classroom: Integrating peacemaking throughout the day

1. A classroom community based on equality, including use of informal and formal conflict resolution techniques and clearly understood guidelines (determined jointly by children and adult);
2. Commitment to community-building with repeated emphasis on children as unique, special people who are all interdependent, interconnected peacemakers;
3. Anti-bias, including race, gender and differently-abled understanding and celebration. Developing relationships with people of all abilities, colors, classes and genders. Celebrating diverse heritages. Coed play encouraged;
4. Study of great peacemakers from many cultures;
5. Care of the Earth, including deep ecology (developing a love of the earth), the three Rs, (reduce, reuse, recycle), gardening, study of endangered species, animal care, valuing all species;
6. Math and science activities that show relationships, and illustrate the grandeur, challenges and interconnectedness of all life;
7. Regular access to, and participation in outdoor nature activities;
8. Care of the classroom, including jobs, cleanup, care of materials;
9. Humor and fun, including cooperative games. Helping children discover alternatives to war play;
10. Peace stories and writing, including rewriting stories to find alternatives to violence, journaling personal peacemaking activities and thoughts, and writing to political leaders. Developing media literacy -- recognizing violence and commercialism, interviewing and reporting on peace efforts;
11. Expressive arts with peacemaking themes, including music, drama, gift-making, drawing, painting, weaving, sculpting, banner/flag-making, peace quilt making, etc.;
12. Peace festival celebrations;
13. Affirmation and friendship activities;
14. Providing peacemaking skill parent education through meetings, workshops and/or newsletters, and warmly welcoming parent involvement;
15. Visual displays of peace, i.e. bulletin boards, posters, children's artwork, pictures of people of different cultures working together, peaceful images such as pictures of beautiful scenery, kindness and cooperation, poems, peace flags, and quotations of peacemakers;
16. Reflection activities;
17. A teaching style which addresses the needs of all learning styles and focuses on the positive;
18. Social action and service with age-appropriate projects.

Peace Is All Around Us. . . Seeing Peace

How do we help children see peace? First we need to help ourselves see peace!

Our ability to see peace can be blunted by the abundance of media-portrayed violent images, the rush of our day-to-day existence, the challenges of making ends meet, supporting a family, planning for our children's future, coping with illness and suffering, and so on and so on. It may seem quite a challenge to begin to discover peace "all around us."

A common approach is to put off peace until we go on vacation, get that promotion, have our work all done, retire, see our children leading successful lives, or purchase some new labor-saving device! Peace seems to be in the future and *conditional*. However, when we practice the art of *mindfulness -- being present in the moment --* there are hundreds of ways to see and experience peace.

Look around you and identify all that is peaceful. You will soon discover peace expressed in countless ways. Perhaps you notice the dew on a rose leaf petal, a stranger letting another car ahead, a child smiling at you, the sunset unfolding, or migrating birds chorusing far over your head.

Peacemakers *look to create peace* rather than waiting for "peace to happen." Peace is an active process! It can be fun and exciting, and more entertaining than violent images.

Some researchers say unless peacemakers can continue to find beauty and peace in their daily lives, three to five years is a typical length of time they are able to remain actively involved, before becoming burned-out, since it is easy to become overwhelmed by the abundance of violence and oppression in the world.

The most powerful act anyone can do for peace is to continue to see it, share it and live it. One's whole life can become a catalyst for creating a more peaceful world. As more and more of us do this, children will be surrounded by powerful peacemaker role models, and begin to increase their abilities to see peace.

Instead of thinking about doing the laundry while having a cup of tea . . . Have a cup of tea! Feel the warmth of the cup on your hands, breathe in the fragrance of the steaming tea leaves, be aware of the sensation spreading through your body as you swallow, and let yourself experience the awe of all the preparation necessary by Mother Earth and various people to make this moment possible. Realize that the tea is connected to you, and to all of life. The tea was grown in the sun and the rain. The sun and rain also are essential for the people who grew, tended and harvested the tea. Your tea was dependent upon them. They are dependent on the same things you depend on. The intricate web of life weaves on.

A walk can become more than getting your daily exercise. Thich Nhat Hanh says to caress the earth with your feet as you walk. (This is much easier to do if you are able to walk directly on the earth rather than sidewalks.) Send appreciative thoughts back to the earth through your feet in gratitude for the gift of life and sustenance. Celebrate the richness of nature surrounding you.

Simple things, even daily grooming, can become peaceful experiences. When washing your face in the morning, see and celebrate all your ancestors. . . their lives, and their struggles making your life possible. While bathing or taking a shower, send love to yourself. Send love to your heart. It beats faithfully for you day in and day out. Send love to your lungs for taking in oxygen. Send love to your liver for filtering the toxins of everyday living. Your organs will benefit tremendously from this kind of compassion and you will feel peace travel throughout your body.

Choose various everyday events you can use as bells or signals to remind you to live in the present moment rather than the past or the future. Some people choose a red traffic light, a ringing telephone, or even the garage door opening to bring them back to mindfulness. Choose signals that are common in your life.

Designing the Environment for Peace

To support our ability to see peace, it's important to spend time with people who practice peace (and live close by for frequent contact, or are just a phone call away). Ask some of them to share their time in your classroom. Study the lives of great peacemakers. How do they maintain their peace of mind? Attend regional and national conferences that include peace education opportunities. Designate at least one in-service or educational opportunity a year for further development of your peacemaking skills.

Designate your school or home as a "peace site," to bring conscious effort to weaving peacemaking activities throughout your curriculum year after year.[1] Develop a peace studies section within your school library or home, so children, parents and teachers have supportive resource material. Learn about the issues of your school and/or neighborhood and develop service and social action projects with the children that make the school and/or neighborhood a more peaceful place to live, work and play.

Once you can see, study and practice peaceful ways of living, you will unleash your creativity and increase your ability to create peaceful experiences and environments for children.

Resources:
[1] For more information about becoming a peace site contact: World Citizen Inc., 2028-B Ford Parkway, Suite 124, St. Paul, MN 55116.

Additional reading:
Avoiding Burnout and Increasing Your Motivation, avail. through The Learning Shop, 706 S. Gammon Rd. Madison, WI.

T. Moore. *Care of the Soul* (1992). Harper Collins.

S. Smith Jones, *Choose to Live Peacefully.* Celestial Arts Publishing, PO Box 7327, Berkeley, CA 94704.

R.C. Arneh, *Dwell in Peace: Applying Nonviolence to Everyday Relationships* (1979). Brethren Press, 1451 Dundee Ave, Elgin, IL 60120.

T. N. Hahn, *Being Peace* (1987). Parallax.

U. Thrush, *Peace 101: The Introduction of Peace as a Mandatory Subject of the Montessori Teacher,* Montessori School of the Golden Gate, 20 Woodside Ave., San Francisco, CA 94127.

It takes some time and thought to design your environment for peace. The task can seem overwhelming if it is viewed as something to "finish" right away. Designing the environment for peace is ongoing work -- we are never finished! New ideas and physical and emotional transformations are part of a continual journey.

Before you begin, include the children in the design process. This is a wonderful starting place for creating the experience of "community." When children are included in the brainstorming process of what could be done to make the room more peaceful, they share their valuable perspectives, as well as begin to develop a sense of belonging and inclusion.

Children's exposure to violent images far outweighs their exposure to peaceful ones. The American Academy of Pediatrics reports that American television and movies are the most violent in the world, and points out that over 1,000 studies show that exposure to heavy doses of television violence increases the likelihood of aggressive behavior, particularly in males. To ameliorate the long-term effects of TV violence, it's important to begin with young children. They need to know that violence is not the "norm."[1] Developing peace as the "standard" takes a commitment to peace, and time.

Show children peaceful scenes
Show children peaceful scenes from nature, people from all cultures working joyfully with each other, adults nurturing children, children nurturing each other, gardens and the fall harvest, animals caring for their young, etc. Develop a collection of these images. Mount them on construction paper, laminate, and display them on the classroom walls and in the hallways. Change them weekly or bi-weekly, so children will not grow too accustomed to them to "see" them. The children can look through various magazines, old calendars and greeting cards for peaceful images and make a scrapbook or a "Peace Is All Around Us," mural to hang in the hallway.

[1] See N. Carlsson-Paige and D. Levin *Who's Calling the Shots? Children's Fascination with War Play* (Washington DC: NAEYC, 1988).

Incorporate peace symbols used around the world into the classroom environment and art activities; doves, rainbows, peace signs, the word "peace" written in many different languages, peace cranes, peace totem poles, earth flags, and so on.

The photograph of Earth taken from space is an image not available to any previous generation. It shows the beauty and limits of our global system. It allows us to see the oneness that unifies the abundant diversity of life forms and human cultures that inhabit this planet.

Periodically, ask the children to look around the classroom community, and identify all things that promote peace, i.e. plants, animals, a vase of flowers, peace posters, displayed art work from students with peace themes, items that celebrate different cultures, pictures of peacemakers, and so on. Discuss what makes these items peaceful in their eyes.

Softness and order

Having pillows, plants, natural lighting, soft drapes or curtains and interesting nooks and crannies helps children feel more peaceful and relaxed. Keeping your environment orderly, with a place for everything, is important, since clutter tends to shut children down, and/or scatter their thinking which may result in agitated behavior. Use moderation in putting things on the walls to prevent children with hyperactivity from becoming overstimulated.

Community gatherings

Ask the children to help you choose a peaceful place to have community time. Explain that this is where we will be talking, sharing and making decisions together. After you and the children have decided where the best place might be for everyone to gather, put a line of tape on the floor (mystic tape will not leave a residue on tile or carpet) in the shape of a circle. The line helps the children easily settle in for gathering time because it's clear where to sit, and they each can be seen and heard. Choosing a circle shape for gatherings also helps establish equality with the group because there is no beginning or end to a circle, and no "head" (if the adult sits in a variety of locations at each gathering time).

Many of us are very sensitive to sound, so the method you use to gather the children sets the tone for community time. We have found it very effec-tive and calming to call the children with a softly beating drum, in the rhythm of 1-2-3-4 with 1 as the emphasized beat, as we sit on the floor with legs crossed. It also is wonderfully calming to us as teachers, as we concentrate on our own breathing and centering ourselves into a peaceful state-of-mind.

Model the way you would like the children to come together. Instead of, "Come here children, it's group time," try just going to the circle, softly beating the drum, centering yourself, and encouraging those who begin to gather to take a place on the community circle. Breathe. After all the children and adults find a spot to sit just behind the line, end the drum beating with a distinct 1-2-3. Continue to model a few moments of silence and breathing. Greet the children in a friendly manner and express your joy in being able to be together again. (Drums with a rich, soothing sound can be purchased at Native American stores, or through Growing Communities for Peace™).

While we model a crossed leg posture, some children may feel more comfortable or centered if they lay on their stomachs with their elbows on the circle line. Children will let you know what they need.

Animals and plants

Because children have a great capacity to give love as well as receive love, it's important to provide avenues for giving love on a daily basis. Having animals and plants helps children demonstrate compassion and empathy. Caring for plants and animals can be posted on a job chart.

If you are hesitant in having animals in your environment because you lack knowledge in how to care for them, we recommend *Animals in the Classroom* by David C. Kramer. Celebrating nature and bringing it indoors is beautifully described in *The Nature Corner* by M.V. Leeuwen and J. Moeskops.

According to John Robbins in *Diet For A New America*,[1] 90% of people in prison abused animals as children. Additionally, studies have shown that prisoners who have been given an animal to care

[1] J. Robbins, *Diet for a New America* (Walpole, New Hampshire, 1987).

for a few months before their release and have been allowed to keep the animals, were less likely to commit another crime. The prisoner receives unconditional love which can motivate him or her to develop a sense of love and caring for another living being.

We've found a fish tank can have a calming, quieting effect on children. By placing it on a low shelf with two-inch bricks, the children can lay on their stomachs while watching the fish. Many children become very relaxed.

If you have the opportunity to design the construction of your own building or your own room, have the windows low to the floor so children can enjoy observing nature. Provide food for birds or squirrels, so they can learn how to feed outdoor animals.

Definition of personal space
The technique of defining a specific work space for each child encourages respect for property and for others. Children learn not to rush in on another's work, but to ask to be invited to join. Having a specific work space also helps the adult invite the child who needs help selecting or putting away work.

Small plain rugs provide each child with a peaceful, well-defined and visually uncluttered work space. Children learn how to unroll a rug when they want to work on the floor and roll it up when they are finished. The rolled rugs can be stored horizontally, in a clothes basket or vertically, in a specially designed rug holder. It's important to teach children how to roll and place rugs, including how to carry them, and how to walk carefully around another's space to avoid disturbing someone's work.

Plastic place-mats serve the same purpose when children are choosing to work at a table. They also help keep the tables clean and free from glue, markers, etc. Children can be shown how to wipe off their mats with a damp sponge before returning them to the shelf. With your help, they can make their own place-mats by preparing two peace drawings which you lightly glue back-to-back, cover with clear contact paper (about an inch bigger all the way around than the drawings) and trim (so there is no stickiness remaining on any edge).

Peace library
Choose a spot in the room for the library that will be a peaceful, quiet, warm and inviting place. The library can be made from something as simple as a plastic crate turned on it's side, a shelf of bricks and boards, or you can purchase a tiered library rack. Peace book topics may include, but are not limited to, self esteem, nature or care of the earth, friendship, great peacemakers, conflict resolution or alternatives to violence, multicultural or ethnic stories, and even stories of peace written and/or illustrated by the children themselves. For a comprehensive guide to peace resources, including those with limited distribution, see Rebecca Janke's *Annotated Guide to Peacemaking Resources*, available through Growing Communities for Peace™.

Bulletin boards
We encourage the use of a bulletin board, large or small. It's a perfect place to celebrate and communicate the peacemaking activities of the children. If you don't have a bulletin board, just use wall space.

Some teachers like to change the bulletin board weekly. Here are some suggestions for the first month:
Week one, the children can draw a picture of a peacemaking activity they have done with or for another person. (Even three-year-olds are able to tell how they have helped someone. The younger children's drawings may not be representational. However, the adult can write down what the child shares about his/her drawing, right on the drawing, so the child, the class, and the family have a record.)

Week two, the theme may be, "Great Peacemakers We Know." The children can draw and/or write about why this person is a peacemaker. (Moms, dads, grandmas and friends are popular for this week's drawing. Later on, you can partner pictures of the children's peacemakers with pictures of historical peacemakers. The historical or famous peacemakers stories can be posted by their pictures.)

Week three, the children can draw, "A Peaceful Place To Be" picture. (Seeing their drawings allows the adult to become more familiar with the child's perspective of peace.)

Week four, the children can cut around their hands, cut them out and make the letters P-E-A-C-E from the cutouts. Put the word PEACE on the bulletin board. The children may want to add doves or folded peace cranes in the upper left and lower right hand corners. (Instructions for folding a peace crane are in many origami books, available in children's stores.)

Continue to choose a different theme each week. Further into the year, children can post their nonviolent responses to conflicts they have resolved with each other or their families, to celebrate that they are getting to be powerful peacemakers!

Another bulletin board can be posted to contain continually updated peace news that the teacher, parents or students clip from newspapers and magazines. These stories can be paraphrased for the younger children. We often complain about the violence depicted in the media, but don't always remember to celebrate the good news. By clipping positive stories and "good news" of peace and justice, children can learn important values.

Music
Research shows we learn new skills more easily through music and stories than through direct instructional methods. Additionally, peacemaking music lets children feel that they are not alone in their peacemaking journey. Peace music helps to counter the culture of violence.

Some singers focusing on peacemaking or care of the earth to look for in addition to *Peacemaker^SM*, are Red Grammer, Sally Rogers, Tom Chapin, Holly Near, Sarah Pirtle, and John McCutcheon.

Also, playing peaceful background music, while the children are working, provides a calming effect. Upbeat music is often not effective for background music. It's preferable to use selections from classical music, sounds of nature, flute or other soothing music. Familiar, upbeat, catchy tunes may provide some very active children with a focal point, however, and can be effective at soothing and calming them. Each classroom responds differently to background music. Explore through observation which music has the most calming effect for your children.

It's ideal if children can turn on peacemaking music with headphones, when they wish. They can then meet their own individual auditory needs.

Sony makes an excellent tape recorder that can be used by the children. It can be ordered from Music For Little People, P.O. Box 1460, Redway, CA 95560-1460. This tool created a peace listening center to listen to stories and music which emphasize peace.

Children want peace tapes played over and over again and sometimes want to enjoy them at home. Therefore, we often encourage parents to purchase them for birthday or holiday presents.

Job chart
On a colorful piece of tag board, or large pizza pie cardboard, make a list of the various jobs to care for the classroom or home environment. Leave enough space on one side (or outside of a circular chart) to put clothespins with the children's names next to each job. Explain, "Being a peacemaker means taking loving care of things and making our home or classroom beautiful and ready for ourselves and others."

If there are more children than jobs, put the extra children's clothespins in a jar. At the end of the week take the last clothespin off the chart and put it in a different jar. Move all the other names down one space and take a child's name from the first jar and put it on the job list. Eventually everyone will have had a job in the environment. A ready-made chart, called the *Job Pocket Chart* is available from the Learning Shop. Your classroom helpers can easily identify their tasks with this 28' by 28' pocket chart. (Grades PreK-3). Sharing jobs also helps build community, since children can see how individual efforts create a collective outcome.

Small bell
Put a bell on a tiny, cloth-covered tray for the children to ring softly if the room becomes too noisy for them. Some children are more sensitive to noise then others, and this enables them to request others to lower their voices and keep the environment peaceful. No words are necessary when you teach the children the sound of the bell means, "let's return to our peace."

Womb spaces
These are soft enclosed areas that children may self-select when they need some alone or quiet time. It can be a industrial-sized plastic drum, carpeted on the inside, a three-sided reading corner, or a three-

sided quiet work area. A womb effect is created by having a low ceiling and limited space. This also can be achieved by hanging a sheet, fishnet, parachute or other material down to about a 4.5 foot level. Womb spaces often prevent acting out behaviors related to stress.

It's important to respect children's need to use these spaces. Sometimes we forget that our busy days may not only be overwhelming to us, but often can be to the children too.

Shelving

Child-size, two-tiered, inexpensive shelving can be made from sanded plywood (that is painted or varnished), or from ready-to-go shelving, mounted on patio bricks.

Children become more self-motivated and self-directed when they have easy access to materials that are displayed simply, and arranged attractively on shelves. It also encourages respect for materials, since each one has a special place on the shelf.

Do your best to provide attractive, complete materials. Often, all that is needed to create interest in an activity or material is to make it attractive/interesting by putting it in a unique basket or putting a piece of colored felt on a tray that matches the work on the tray. Children become frustrated by incomplete materials. At the end of each day, check for any missing pieces of equipment. If they cannot be found, take the work off the shelf until they are found or replaced.

Rotating opportunities to work with materials often decreases discipline problems because the children stay interested, challenged and focused on their work. This applies in the family home as well. Implementing a materials rotation also helps maximize the mileage from each piece of equipment.

Peace candle

Light a candle for special ceremonies or group problem solving as a reminder to let our love shine. Help the children understand the power in choosing to let their love or peace shine.

Peace corner with shelf

This is a place for "sacred objects" such as the talking stick, the Good Heart Journal, a peace candle, symbols of peace, and so on. It becomes a classroom space that children revere and respect. Some children like to go to this place when they feel a need to center themselves or enjoy their inner peace.

Periodically, ask the children for additional ideas for the peace corner. They may even begin to bring items spontaneously, as will their parents, when they realize that this is the focus of the environment. When this begins to happen, you know integration is taking place.

Peacemaker Puppet™

Whatever we focus on expands and becomes our reality. The reality children want to experience is living in a peaceful world. Therefore, it is vitally important that children role play their ideas and experiences of peace. When shown alternatives to violence, children will readily use these tools for portraying stories of peace. Hearing stories of peacemakers encourages them to pretend to be these people in their dramatic play.

The *Peacemaker Puppet™* is designed so young children can learn to focus on peace and nonviolence. The puppet is instrumental in helping children practice supportive, caring language, resolve conflicts, express feelings in an appropriate manner, find alternatives to violence, perform service projects, become involved in age-appropriate social action, care for others, and create new stories of peace.

We retain what we learn through our stories, music, and hands-on experiences. This makes the *Peacemaker Puppet™* a valuable educational aid for children. The Puppet helps children internalize nonviolent living skills. It can be used by teachers, parents or the children. (Available through Growing Communities for Peace™).

Peace quote and affirmation mirror

At the entrance to the classroom, home or center, have a mirror with different peace quote signs on it each week. One sign might say, "Let peace begin with me." Children can be invited to stand and look in the mirror with their own face above the word "me." Other ideas are "I'm a peacemaker," "Here is a peacemaker," "We can work it out," and "Peacemakers care about each other." Children like to repeat positive affirmations about themselves such as "I am a special person," "I am

good at. . . " and "I can cool off when I'm angry."
You can make up many more or find inspiration
from short quotes by famous peacemakers. Children will spontaneously develop their own peace
quotes and affirmations which promote healthy self-
talk. (See *Additional Reading* *at the end of this*
section.)

Invite people of the community to visit

People who have jobs at the water department,
government offices, fire department, veterinary
clinic, health clinic, dentist's office, food co-op,
grocery store, police station, mediation center,
parks and recreation center, etc., can be introduced
as *peacemakers of your particular city or town.*
They can share with the students how, as peacemakers, they make the city a better place to live, work
and play. Be sure to emphasize to the children that
these people go to work every day to do this peacemaking work, and talk about how grateful we are for
their efforts.

Small group snack table

In early childhood settings, some children are
hungry before snack time. Perhaps they missed
breakfast. Setting up a snack table encourages the
children to eat according to their individual needs,
thus preventing hunger, a physical stressor, leading
to acting out behaviors from low blood sugar.

Putting out a card, with the correct number of snack
items that may be eaten, helps the children to eat the
right amount so there is enough for everybody.
Putting a piece of tape on the floor for two children
to "wait" on, prevents many children from racing to
empty snack chairs. Thus, you will have two
children at the snack table, and two children waiting
while the rest of the children continue to work until
there is an empty place at the tape line.

Use a small pitcher so children can pour their own
juice successfully. Napkins can be used as "plates."
Show them how to fold the four corners of the
napkin, into the center of the napkin so any crumbs
stay inside it.

Have a garbage can and compost container next to
the snack table for disposing of their waste paper
and food, respectively. Helping children clearly
understand the reason for separating their waste, so
they know the connection between the snack
leftovers and the rejuvenation of the garden soil,

provides the necessary motivation for cleaning up in
a loving manner.

In Gratitude
by Julie Penshorn Peterson, 1994

In gratitude, each step I walk, I try
To step, lightly so my Earth won't die.
Recall, how she keeps giving each day
Gifts for us all, in limitless ways.
With others too, our service we give,
And we live lightly, so all life can live.

Place a small bucket with warm sudsy water and a
sponge near the snack area for the children to clean
up any spills. (We call this the "Whoops" bucket.)
Rather than berating children for accidental spills,
we teach them that if they spill they just need to get
the "whoops" bucket, and clean up.

A peacemaker is someone who shows gratitude.
Therefore, before eating, the children can be invited
to have a moment of silence for giving thanks to the
people who helped plant the food, for those who
harvested it, for those who made it into a snack, or
for Mother Earth. They may also give a specific
wish for peace in their classroom, families, neighborhood or world. Be sure to explain this practice
to the parents so that they don't become concerned
that a particular religion is being practiced.

Provide dress-up clothes

Dress-up clothes for different occupations can lead
children to role play local peacemakers such as
doctors, nurses, dentists, fire-fighters, grocery
clerks, and so on. Encourage them to portray these
roles showing how these people make the community a better place to live. Be careful to be gender-
fair, and not refer to the doctor as "he" or the nurse
as "she." Watch the children for gender stereotyp-
ing, and address it through discussion and demonstration (invite a male nurse to visit, a female police
officer, and so on). Career Characters Dress Up
Dolls and Career Costume Sets can be obtained
from Lakeshore Learning Materials. Call 800-421-
5354 for their catalog. Career puppets and Community Action Figures also are available from

Lakeshore. These materials also may be purchased from ABC School Supply, at 800-669-4222.

Invite the students to create a peace village
Blocks, Legos, Tinker Toys or any combination of things make wonderful peace villages. Older children enjoy clay, papier-mache, or wood. Encourage children to think about: What will it look like? How will the people solve their problems? What kind of games will they play? How will they keep the rivers and lakes clean? How will people treat each other?

This is a good opportunity to integrate the boys and girls in an activity, since often the boys will be readily involved with construction projects, and the girls might prefer to play with the construction after it is built. (This has been the experience of researchers at Legos). The peace village, where everyone can contribute to the whole, and explore their own unique interests, involves cooperation, and develops teamwork.

Experiencing inner peace
Introduce the Silence Game. (See *Other Ideas for Building Community*, page 23) Learn how to "be still." Make silence before going to work in the classroom. Invite children to close their eyes for a few seconds to feel their inner peace. This activity, done regularly, increases their ability to become peaceful on their own, and helps their attention span and concentration. It also helps them realize that being quiet is meaningful, interesting, and even fun, rather than a painful experience associated with inactivity, punishment, or an adult's needs.

Peace tree
Put a fallen branch with several twigs on it into a coffee can with plaster and let it harden. This becomes the Peace tree. (Alternatively, draw a picture of a tree on paper on the wall, or invite the children to help make a portion of the tree. Each child can add a branch and some leaves.) Children can hang different items on it according to the peace theme of the week. (They can be attached to the wall version with push pins.) Some ideas are small drawings of endangered animals, a leaf-shape cutout depicting an act of kindness, a cutout drawing of their favorite peacemaker symbols such as doves, rainbows, hearts or clouds. Even mittens or hats can be put on it to give to the local shelter for homeless

children. The children will delight in coming up with other ideas. Encourage children to visit the area near the peace tree, when they want to think about peace, or get back to peace.

Hug-a-planet soft globe
Suspend this from the ceiling so the children can hug Mother Earth whenever they want. Put up a sign on the wall near the globe that says, "Come Hug Mother Earth." Soft huggable globes of the world in various sizes are available through XTC Products, 247 Rockingham, Avenue, Larchmont, NY 10538.

The peace pole project
Peace poles have been dedicated the world over as an international symbol of peace. Their purpose is to spread the message, "May Peace Prevail on Earth," and act as constant reminders of the necessity to work for peace at all times. Peace poles carry this message of peace to stimulate our desire for peace. For more information write: The Peace Pole Project, 3534 Lanham Road, Maple City, MI 49664 or call 616-334-4567.

Multicultural center
Have a flat map, with removable pieces, of the world's continents. Children can learn the names of the continents and their shapes by tracing them on construction paper and punching them out. Using a push pin, children poke the pin through the boundary of the traced continent paper at small intervals (using a small carpet mat under their work). The smaller the intervals are made, the easier it is to "punch" out. The continents are placed on a large piece of blue construction paper, representing the oceans, and the children label the continents and the oceans so they have their own world map.

We've seen many PreK-3 children get excited about making a world citizen vest after they know the names of all the continents. The vest can be made (by parent volunteers) from blue felt, representing the oceans. The continents are made from felt as well, and are in the same colors as the continents of the map being used. The continents are glued on the front and back of the vest. When a child is able to name all the continents, he or she receives a vest and is celebrated as a "world citizen" at a special ceremony at the closing community time of the day. A world citizen, the children learn, finds ways to know and care about people all over the world.

To avoid taking a "tourist" approach to the many cultures of the world, we suggest inviting people from different cultures to spend some time in your setting. Ask the guests to talk about the various customs and some history of their culture. Encourage them to bring pictures and artifacts to share. The children can feel and experience peace from these one-on-one interactions. Children develop a deeper appreciation and respect, and experience a loss of fear, with these heart connections. Without developing one-to-one relationships with people, multicultural studies become only intellectual exercises, and are far less meaningful for the children. After these visits, study that particular culture for several months in order to explore it more deeply.

You and the children can cut out magazine pictures relating to the aspects of life in your focus culture. You can mount them on construction paper and laminate if you wish. Post them on the wall and put some of them into a pocket folder for children to study in the reading corner. Get books at the library featuring people from this area of the world, or cultural background. Role play the stories the children resonate to.

Writing for Peace
Peace post office

Young children can send each other pictures or gifts they have made with a post office cubby with all the names of the children. This gives the children an additional avenue to show they care about each other.

Older children can use the U.S. Postal Service as their peace post office for peace pen pals in other countries or to write letters to government leaders. Contact Peace Links, 729 8th Street SE, Suite 300, Washington, DC 20003 or phone (202) 544-0805 for pen pals.

Roots and Wings catalog, P.O. Box 350, Jamestown, CO 84055, has a beautiful Earth rubber stamp that children can use as a logo or personal mark on stationary or envelopes.

Partnership stories through the mail

Another way to use the mail for peace is the through the Partnership Stories Project of Parents, Teachers and Students for Social Responsibility, Inc., PO Box 517, Moretown, Vermont 05660. The Partnerships Stories Project was developed as a tool for learning about other cultures and peoples. This project, which is appropriate for any age or grade level, enlists at least two groups of young people from different countries. One group writes the first

Finding Positive Behaviors
in the Midst of Challenging Behaviors

Sometimes the behavior of children causes us to ask: "Will they ever be peace-makers?" Focusing on looking for the positive in as many behaviors as possible, helps us remain peaceful, and helps children maintain their dignity and respect, as they learn to master their skills.

A ratio of 4:1 is the minimum positive to negative comment ratio necessary for children to *maintain existing emotional strength. A ratio of 12:1 is necessary for behavior improvement.* When the ratio is 20:1 the home or classroom becomes a peaceful environment for all.[1]

Positive comments can simply be words of support and encouragement. For example: A bed that is poorly made is an opportunity to turn a criticism into a positive comment such as: "I see you made the bed all by yourself."

A painting excursion onto a wall of the school or home can be met with: "I see you want to paint on a big place. Because we can't paint on the walls, I will show you where we can paint on something big, after we wash them off."

[1] Jon Bell, behavioral consultant, Somerset, Wisc. "A Twenty-five Year Participatory Research Report: How Much Praise is Enough?" (Unpublished manuscript.)

part of a story which is later completed or resolved by a second group. The partnership story groups develop relationships with one another by exchanging stories, letters, photographs, and cassette tapes. The first partnership story, a Soviet-American tale entitled, *The Monkey's Dilemma,* was published in 1990. Children from all over the world are now co-writing stories. The Partnership Stories Project received the endorsement of the Vermont National Education Association.

The Good Heart Journal: Recording Positive Behaviors

Children seem to love to tattle. Some tattle because they think it might be a way to obtain revenge. Others use it as a means of getting attention.

Using a Good Heart Journal causes children to focus on positive qualities and behaviors of themselves and others. The following activity is appropriate for any school, daycare or preschool setting, but can also be very effective in the home. Using a three-ring-binder containing notebook paper and labeled, "Good Heart Journal," your community can have an opportunity, each day, to record the good deeds members have done.

We bring the book to our closing ceremony each day. Gather the children around you and ask them what peacemaking behavior they saw or did that was helpful, kind, caring or loving.   Record their answers and/or invite the children to draw or paint some of them. They can be added to the binder. Write the descriptions for them if they are non-writers.

You might like to add something *you* saw the children or yourself do. Each time you do a peacemaking lesson, the Good Heart Journal can be used for reflection, celebration and review of the lesson goals.

A Story: Finding Ivan's Positive Behavior

Judy, a child care provider who is committed to peacemaking, had been reading from Terrence Webster-Doyle's book, *Facing the Double-Edged Sword: The Art of Karate for Young People*[1], because she appreciated the author's belief that in order for children or adults to be able to be nonviolent, they must not be ruled by their fears.   She was learning that reducing fear depends on becoming educated in peacemaking skills, practicing alternatives to violence, and having confidence that you can defend yourself without weapons.

Webster-Doyle's book also appealed to her because he taught the children that the goal of a karate master -- who trained with the ancient philosophy of karate, rather than the commercialized version -- was *never* to fight, but instead to use a nonviolent alternative. It was a very sad occasion when fighting was necessary to protect oneself. The children had begun to peacefully experiment with karate, though no one was taking formal lessons.

She had repeatedly emphasized Webster-Doyle's nonviolent philosophy to the children, and thus was dismayed when six-year-old Ivan, a kindergartner who came to her house for after-school care, announced with pride that he had gotten into a fight on the bus, and had used a karate sidekick on the older girl who was bothering him! Rather than quickly jumping to conclusions that he hadn't heard a word about nonviolence, she asked him if he had made physical contact with the older girl with his sidekick. "No," he said, "I just pretended to kick her."

Judy, looking for the positive said, *"Ivan, it seems you are beginning to understand nonviolence from the book we are reading together. You didn't hurt her. It's wonderful that you were able to control yourself. I wonder what the book will say today about nonviolence when someone wants to have a fight with us?"*

[1] T. Webster-Doyle, *Facing the Double Edged Sword: The Art of Karate for Young People*, (Atrium Press, Box 938, Ojai, CA 93023, 1988) **Other books by T. Webster-Doyle**: *Fighting the Invisible Enemy: The Effects of Conditioning on Young People; Why is Everybody Always Picking on Me? A Guide to Handling Bullies for Young People; Tug of War: Peace Through Understanding Conflict.Looking for Positive Behavior.*

Keep this book accessible at all times. Children enjoy looking at it like other special books, but find it even more fascinating because it is representative of their community's life together. Parents love looking at it as well, and it helps them understand what you and the children value.

Interested children can make a Good Heart Journal to take home as a family gift. Coupled with a note of explanation about how to use the Journal, this is an opportunity for the child to teach his or her family about peacemaking skills. Some family members may not participate, but the child's gift may serve as an inspiration to the family to increase their focus on the positive. Families might use this at dinner time, or as a bedtime ritual. They child can make their own contribution to the journal, and then ask the parent(s), "What would *you* (or other family members) like to add to the Good Heart Journal tonight?"

Each day of the week (or each week) a different child can be invited to be a peace reporter. He or she is invited to look for "peace events" in the classroom and/or school, and is free to report back in any medium, such as videotape, oral story, written story, collage, pantomime, skit, sculpture, and so on to the community. These reports can be shared with the entire school at a peace festival.

Additional Reading: Design of the Environment
J. Greenman, *Caring Spaces, Learning Places: Children's Environments that Work,* Scholastic, PO Box 7502, Jefferson City, MO 65102.
E. Jensen, *Optimal Learning Environment* (1994). Turning Point.
L. Derman Sparks, *Anti-Bias Curriculum*, published by NAEYC, Washington DC.bers) like to add to the Good Heart Journal tonight?"
M. J. Parks, *Peacemaking for Little Friends* (1985). Little Friends for Peace, 4405 29th St, Mt. Rainer MD 20712

Posters for Your Environment
Peace Posters, NAEYC, 1824 Connecticut Ave NW, Washington, DC 20009
Self Esteem Poster Set, Lakeshore Learning Materials, 2695 E Dominguez St., Carson, CA 90749.
Rainforest Posters, Tricylce Press, PO Box 7123 Berkeley, CA 94707

Additional Reading: Writing for Peace
G.G. Jampolsky (ed.), *Children As Teachers of Peace*, Celestial Arts, PO Box 7327, Berkeley, CA 94707.
L. King and D. Stovall, *Classroom Publishing*, Zephyr Press.
Macintosh Software, *Easy Book*, Prufrock Press, PO Box 8813, Waco, TX 76714.
J. Whitfield (1994). *Getting Kids Published*, Prufrock.
Ground Zero Resource Center, *Global Ladder*, PO Box 19329, Portland, OR.
S. Fluck, *How to Organize a Peace Essay Contest in Your Community,* Peace Education Resoruce Center.
J. Larson and M. Micheals-Cryus (eds., 1987). *Seeds of Peace* New Society, PO Box 582, Santa Cruz, CA 95061.

Additional Reading: Focusing on the Positive
D and J. Loomans (1984). *Full Esteem Ahead*, H. J. Kramer, Inc. PO Box 1082, Tiburon, CA 94920 (PreK-6).
N. Curry and C. Johnson, *Beyond Self Esteem: Developing a Genuine Sense of Human Value*, NAEYC, Washington, DC.
B. Reider, *Hooray Kind of Kid*, Sierra House Pub., 2716 King Richard Drive, El Dorado Hills, CA 95630 (PreK-6).
C. Goode and J. Lehni Watson (1992). *Mind Fitness*, Zephyr Press, 3316 N. Chapel Ave. PO Box 13448, Tucson, AZ 85732.
J. Canfield and H. C. Wells, *100 Ways to Enhance Self-Concept in the Classroom*.
M. Avery & D. Avery, *What is Beautiful* (1995). Tricycle Press, PO Box 7123 Berkeley, CA 94707.

I Love it When
by Julie P. Peterson, 1995

I love it when we can make peace
It always seems so right
To find a way to give and take
So things come out all right.

I love it when I'm listened to;
When I share with my words.
It seems I'm much more peaceful,
When I know that I've been heard.

I love it when we get ideas. . .
Though they at first feel bad
Then we think and think some more,
And find one better than we had!

I love it when we work it out --
Between many or just two.
'Cause when we put ideas together,
One and one makes more than two.

Introduction

The underlying premises for this chapter are:

1. Children desire a loving, supportive community;
2. Teachers can help empower children;
3. It is possible to prevent, reduce, or work through conflict with developed communication skills;
4. Peacemaking skill development goes hand-in-hand with positive attitude and values development, resulting in a more peaceful classroom;
5. Children have great capacity for learning peacemaking skills and understanding and appreciating the benefits of conflict;
6. A great many cultures depend on relationship building and community as key ingredients to conflict resolution.

Creating a peaceful climate, through our tone, our role modeling, our behavior and the design of our physical environment, provides children and adults with a safe place to practice peacemaking skills. We must dare to experiment with our skills in order to improve them, so we can sustain ourselves, our earth and each other.

To build a community of peace with the children, the children must be liberated from the chains of authoritarian rule and yet protected from the chaos of unstructured freedom. The following activities reveal strategies for empowering children.

Respectful group sharing with the talking stick

One way to embrace a multicultural approach in our teaching is to employ tools and methods originating in a variety of cultural traditions, giving credit to the originators. The Native American tradition of passing an artifact around the circle to facilitate group discussions is one example of this approach.

The talking stick originally was used by tribes of Native Americans as a reminder to use words to make important decisions or solve problems, instead of using weapons. It is a tradition that has been passed down over the years and has remained because of its efficacy in helping resolve conflicts in community life. It helps facilitate a variety of group activities, and sets a respectful and caring tone for the community. It can be used throughout the year for group problem solving and community decision-making.

The following *Talking Stick Lesson* begins to set the stage for community to develop among the children. Using this hands-on tool teaches children that groups of people can make decisions without violent words or deeds.

The consensus/consent decision-making process is an important ingredient for creating a peaceful classroom. This process leads to stronger bonds between community members and develops relationships of trust. (Voting, on the other hand, often leads to competition, separation, distrust, and frustration, from unmet needs.) In a consensus decision-making process, everyone has an opportunity to speak his or her mind, and everyone listens carefully, since the more we understand each other, the more capable we are of finding a win-win solution. We may even find a synergistic solution that's better than any we could have found working independently. If someone in the group does not wholeheartedly embrace the decision, in this process, they may choose to block the decision from going forward, or they can "consent," or agree. When they do this, they are saying they aren't 100% pleased, but they aren't going to stop the process from moving forward.

The talking stick is useful to help children begin to trust that they don't need to compete for time and attention to be heard. The "quiet" child and the "talkative" child are both helped with this tool since each person has an equal opportunity to speak. Once they build this trust, listening skills substantially increase. The talking stick becomes a sacred symbol of the group's respectful communication practices, and is a reminder of the value of each member in the community.

In addition, because stories create bonding, while tattling creates division, sharing through the use of the talking stick is an effective way to open discussions. It helps children move directly to expression of feelings, and eliminates a great deal of blaming.

Building Community and the Talking Stick Lessons

Goals:

1. To introduce each person in community, and develop a safe atmosphere
2. To begin to show children that they are in a community of peacemakers, and each of them already do peacemaking behaviors
3. To encourage children to connect with the larger community through the children on the audiotape, who also are peacemakers
4. To empower the children to communicate respectfully in a group
5. To help children realize they don't need to compete for time and attention
6. To communicate that problems can be solved with words, not violence.
7. To reflect on how others have been peacemakers to them

Materials:

1. Peace journals for each child (Assemble 10 sheets of blank paper into a book by folding the sheets in half and stapling one or two times on the fold in the center. Older children can assemble their own journals and put the words, "Peace Journal" on the cover, which can be made of wallpaper or decorated in a variety of ways. Another idea is to copy the picture of *Peacemaker*^{SM} in this book, reducing or enlarging it to fit on the journal covers, and then coloring it in.)
2. Water soluble markers or crayons for each child
3. A fallen branch from a tree (approximately 1" diameter by 14" long)
4. *We Can Solve it Peacefully* audiotape, by *Peacemaker*^{SM}.

Presentation:

1. Begin by gathering the children into a circle on the floor. Welcome them all to the classroom community. Explain: "Good morning! I am _____. Welcome! I am so happy that all of you have come to be part of this class, or *community*. Let's start by getting to know each other."

2. Share an introduction song or game. Any gathering song that is inclusive, friendly, and builds name recognition will work. Here are a couple:
 This is to the tune of *Here We Go Round the Mulberry Bush.*

We're sending smiles to ___
 (child's name)
Sending smiles to ___ (same child's name)
Sending smiles to ___(same child's name)
To welcome him/her today.

You may want to finish this song with this verse:
Sending smiles to all of us, To welcome us today.
Go around the circle and all sing to each child.

In a larger group, a shorter tune works better. Here's another favorite to the tune of *Go Tell Aunt Rhody.*
Good morning <u>Alex</u>
Good morning <u>Andrew,</u>
Good morning <u>Kayla,</u>
Welcome to our class.

Go around the circle, substituting names until all have been included. Don't forget to sing "good morning" to yourself. Shake each child's hand as you sing the song.

3. "I'm so glad we are beginning to know each other. We are a new *community*. Out of my care and concern for us, I would like to talk about how we can be peaceful to each other this year, so this is a safe community. Let's think about ways we already know how to be peacemakers." (Start referring to the children as peacemakers whenever possible.) Invite them to share a few ideas.

4. "I would like to share a song that some children sing about themselves as peacemakers. I will tell you a story about them. These children are lots of

I'm Always the Right Age
by Julie P. Peterson, 1994

I'm only three, and already
I set plates, I can clear,
Put away silverware,
And give a big kiss to my gramma dear.

Chorus:
"Cause I'm always the right age to care.
I'm always the right age to share.
I'm never too young or too old to be kind.
With love in my heart, I've got peace on
 my mind.

I'm only four, just four, no more.
I take baths, I can scrub.
Put myself in the tub.
Help Mom or Dad with the rub-a-dub-
 dub.

I'm only six, I've got some tricks.
I sort trash, take it out,
I'm a recycling scout,
And I teach my friends to help animals
 out.

I'm only eight, but eight is so great!
I make peace, I don't fight
Even when I am right.
I'm a peacemaker, both day and night.

different ages. At first, the younger children thought they couldn't do anything for peace, and the older children said, 'You're too little!' Then, one courageous (or brave) child said, 'I think kids can be peacemakers no matter how old they are. I can help my family, my friends, and the Earth in lots of ways, but even my baby brother is a peacemaker when he smiles. . . And he's especially peaceful when he's sleeping!' So all the children thought about it and discovered they could be peacemakers no matter how young or old they were, because there were lots of things they did that were kind and caring. The children on the tape will sing about some of those things, like setting plates on the table, clearing dishes, putting away the silverware, taking baths, scrubbing up, cooperating with Mom and Dad, and even recycling and getting along with others!" (Play the song: *I'm Always the Right Age to Care* from *Peacemaker's*[SM] audiotape: *We Can Solve it Peacefully*, and/or read it as a poem. This helps children get more ideas about how they already are peacemakers.)

5. "That was fun listening to children singing about being peacemakers. Who would like to share some of the things they do to be peacemakers? (Listen to their stories.)

6. "In a peacemaking classroom, we can get really excited about doing kind and respectful, peace-making things for ourselves, each other, and our Earth! Today I'm going to do a peacemaking behavior. Are you ready?" *Yes!* "O.K. I'm going to give you a *special* book I made for each one of you! This is a Peace Journal. Let's say that:" *Peace Journal.* "These words say, 'Peace Journal.' Our

Peace Journal is a book for recording our ideas about peace.

7. "I would like to invite you to design your cover for peace. Maybe it will show something that is peaceful or a peacemaking behavior you've done. Maybe you want to draw one of the ideas you heard in the song, or maybe you have a completely new idea. It's your journal, so draw anything that seems to be peaceful to you with these crayons (or markers). While we draw, I'll play the song once more, so we get to know it better." (Pass out journals. Play the dialog on the tape right before the song, and the song. You can point out some of the following behaviors to the children if they are having trouble recognizing what they do to be a peacemaker: recycling, helping around the house, feeding the animals, taking care of siblings, kissing mommy or daddy, gardening, planting flowers or trees, and so on.)

8. Asking for specific information about the child's work leads them to further sharing than they might otherwise do. First invite a volunteer: "Who would like to share their drawing with the group? Thank you. Can you tell us which part of your picture you drew first? What else would you like to tell us about your cover on your Peace Journal? . . . Thank you for *sharing* your thoughts. Do you think sharing is a peace-making thing to do?" Yes. "Sure it is! Let's clap for _____ who shared with us."

Second Session:
1. Show the 14" stick and say, "In a peacemaking class we care about what thoughts we each want to share, and what feelings we each have.

"This morning, I was walking outside, and I found this stick. I brought here for us, because it is a peacemaking tool called a *'talking stick.'* Let's take a walk outside (if the weather permits), and I'll tell you a story about how some people found a creative and respectful way to listen to each other's thoughts and feelings." (A ceremony for introducing the talking stick is going outside with the children, and sitting under a tree in a circle. If you prefer, rather than presenting the stick to the children, the class can go for a nature walk and find the stick together. The teacher then tells the following story.)

2. Talking Stick Story
Many, many years ago, there was a lot of fighting between the people of five Native American tribes: the Mohawk, Senaca, Cayuga, Oneida and Onandaga. It was so dangerous that many people had left their homes, and were suffering from starvation. All these tribes lived near the shores of Lake Ontario, in what is now upper New York and southeastern Ontario. They tell a story about a man, named Deganawidah, and his friend, Hiawatha*, who helped them make a peace agreement between the five tribes.

Deganawida came to the land of the five tribes in a stone canoe, which seemed mysterious, since everyone expected a stone canoe to sink. He told the people he met that the "good news of the great peace has come."[1] He was a great peacemaker.

Deganawida announced that he would plant a Great Tree of Peace to help the five tribes find peace. The branches would protect the people, and the white roots of truth would reach out to the four directions,
*Not the Hiawatha of Longfellow's story.

carrying news of peace. He invited the warriors from all the tribes to bury their weapons of war in the ground. Then he planted the tree over the weapons and they sat down to make their *peace agreement*.

They didn't get it done in one day. No. It took years! But finally, they formed the Iroquois Confederacy, or the League of Peace, which continues to this day. (Their peace agreement was so powerful, it inspired the writers of the United States Constitution, the United Nations Charter, and others.)[2]

Deganawidah believed that it was important for each person wishing to speak to be carefully listened to, because everyone's ideas are valuable. When they *listened carefully from their hearts*, and *spoke truthfully from their hearts*, the people were able to make peace.

To help the people work together, Deganawidah brought powerful symbols of peace. One tradition was to pass something important around the circle, to show who was speaking from his or her heart. Some Native Americans began to use a *talking stick* as

A kindergartner using a talking stick

this symbol. They pass the talking stick around the circle when they have *council*. Council is a time for sharing thoughts and feelings about an important subject. When people have council and can talk about their problems, they don't need to have fights or wars anymore. Sometimes it can take a long time to solve a problem, but that's O.K., because when we are patient we can find a solution that shows respect for everyone.

We are the inheritors of a great American legacy: we are the children of Deganawidah. We are the children of Africa, Asia, Europe, the South Pacific and all the Americas, who have come to live under the peace of the great tree. . . We must now nurture the Great Tree and water its white roots of peace.[3]

3. (Pause for a moment, then continue) "We are a *community*, or *tribe* too. Each one of us is special to this community. We need everyone's sharing and everyone's ideas to solve our problems nonviolently, instead of kicking, hitting, biting, calling each other names or not being friends to each other. In a peacemaking class, we respect everyone in our community.

4. "I am a teacher who believes we can solve our *problems* with words, instead of weapons, that's why I brought us a stick today. *WE* can make it into our talking stick. It is so special to us, we even hold it in a special way. . . like this (model holding it with two hands, like kindergartner picture).

5. When the discussion is over, ask the children how they would like to **decorate the talking stick**. Some children like to use items from

nature. Other children might bring little mementoes from home that have special significance. Others might want to use ribbons, bells, or other available items. Older children might want to use a wood burning kit to engrave their names on the stick. The decorating is best if it represents the interests of the members of the community and/or reminds the members of something important and personal for them.

Third Session:
1. "When we come together to solve a problem, and sit in a circle like this, we are having *council*. We use the talking stick to remind ourselves whose turn it is to *speak from the heart* while the rest of us listen deeply from our hearts. It is important not to be thinking about what we're going to say when someone else has the stick. You will have plenty of time to think about what you want to say when you have the stick. We will wait while you get ready to speak.

2. "I'm going to pass the talking stick in *sun direction* or *clockwise*. Remember it's your turn to speak when you have it, and it's your turn to *listen* when someone else has it. When the talking stick comes to you, take a few deep breaths and think about what you would like to say. When you are finished speaking, hold the stick for a

[1.] J. Houston, *Manual for the Peacemaker: An Iroquois Legend to Heal Self & Society* (Quest Books, Wheaton, IL, 1995, p. 20. Highly recommended for adult reading.)

[2] M Caduto & J. Bruchac, *Keepers of Life: Discovering Plants Through Native American Stories and Earth Activities for Children*, (Fulcrum Publishing, Golden, Co, 1994, p. 9).

[3] J. Houston, *Manual for the Peacemaker: An Iroquois Legend to Heal Self & Society* (Quest Books, Wheaton, IL, 1995, p. 146).

moment to make sure there's nothing else you want to say. Then, pass it to the next person in sun direction. If you don't want to say anything you can say, '*Pass*.' You can have another chance to speak after the talking stick goes around the circle to everybody.

3. "To practice using the talking stick, let's each think of a time when someone was a peacemaker to us. What did the person do or say that made you think he or she was being a peacemaker? When the stick comes to you, share your story, or you may say, 'Pass.'

4. "When you speak, the rest of us will listen very deeply to you (lower your voice to a whisper) like we would if we were in the forest listening for an animal. That's how we will show our *respect* to you."

Teaching tips:
It is useful to begin community time together with the children, with a brief check-in to share their current thoughts or feelings. There may be unresolved disputes or troubles brewing that need attention before the group can function well. The teacher might say: "Let's start out today with our check-in. Just describe how you are feeling and what you've been thinking about." The teacher then begins by sharing how he or she is feeling, thus modeling the appropriate use of the talking stick.

When a problem needs to be resolved, the sharing time is even more powerful when someone has a similar story to share from the past and tells how he/she felt at that time. For example, the teacher might say, "There are some people in our class whose

ball is being taken away from them while they are playing catch in the field. So, for today's check-in, I would like to ask anyone to speak who has had a ball taken from them. If anyone has ever taken a ball from someone, they may also speak and tell us how they were feeling and how they came to do that."

After the talking stick has gone around the complete circle and it's evident there is a need for more discussion, place the stick in the middle of the circle. Whoever would like to speak comes to the center of circle, picks it up, speaks, and returns it to the center.

If the council meeting goes too long, children will show signs indicating the meeting needs to end and be resumed at a later time. If this happens, be sure to tell the children something like: "Sometimes all the sharing we do takes a long time. That's O.K. We can be patient and we will learn more about each other. We can stop for a while and come back later. It is important to keep talking until we've heard what everyone has to say."

Suggestions for building community with children:
1. Shake each child's hand and greet him/her upon arrival and departure. Bend or kneel to the child's level and look sincerely into his/her eyes.

2. Be at peace yourself. The children will feel your peacefulness. Your peaceful aura will help children feel calm.
3. Each day, focus on a particular child. Whenever you have a spare minute between activities or during the activities themselves,

get to know this child more deeply. Rotate through your class and then start over again. Some teachers like to journal and record all the positive, peaceful information they learn and observe about the child of the day, and present it as a *Peace Journal from the Teacher* memento at the end of the school year.

The child can be invited to help you with special jobs, tell you a story about him/herself, go first in line, and walk hand-in-hand with you when going from place to place. The spontaneous conversations that will take place create an opportunity for further bonding and give you insight into the skills and talents the child brings to his or her peacemaking journey. You also will learn what obstacles, to realizing his or her full potential, are in the child's path. Having this knowledge, you will be better prepared to bring the necessary resources to the classroom that will meet the needs of individual children.

Empowerment of the Children:
1. Being able to talk without being interrupted
2. Realizing everyone's ideas are important
3. Sharing the ways they are peacemakers
4. Listening to other ways of being a peacemaker
5. Understanding that in community, members can share ideas and listen in a respectful manner

Points of Interest:
1. *I'm Always the Right Age to Care* sung by children
2. The talking stick
3. Being outside
4. Relating in a new way to each other
5. Decorating the talking stick
6. Hearing a story

Language Development:

1. Peacemaker
2. Peacemaking classroom
3. Sharing
4. Native American
5. Peace Journal
6. Community
7. Talking Stick
8. Respect
9. Peace agreement
10. Problem
11. Solution
12. Pass
13. Council
14. Tribe
15. Listen with your heart
16. Speak from your heart

Extensions and Variations:

1. **If you stay inside for the talking stick lesson, use a candle** for your talking stick ceremony, if building regulations permit. The fire on the candle represents the light of goodness in each one of us, and can help us remember to speak and listen from our hearts. A resource on this topic is *Something Special Within,* by Betts Richter (Devorss and Co., CA, PreK-3).

2. **Have a carpenter or older student make a special stand** or case for the talking stick. It can be displayed in a prominent place in the classroom. This symbolizes the community's agreement to solve problems with words, not violence, and to appreciate the members of the community. It also is empowering for the children to know that the talking stick is available whenever they have a problem to work out with the group, or need to be heard.

3. **Experiment** with the children using different tools or artifacts in place of the talking stick. Explain that even if they don't have a talking stick readily available, other items can be used.

4. **Use the talking stick to solve a problem *you* have** with the group. For example, if you are in a family day care setting, you might have this problem: "At lunchtime, I am finding it difficult to prepare the lunch because many children are asking for my attention at that time. What can we do to solve this problem?" Record *all* the ideas. In the lesson on *Choosing a Solution* you will find ways to deal with unworkable suggestions.

Additional Reading for Adults for Building Community

T. Morrison, W.A.Conaway, G.A. Borden, *How to Do Business in Sixty Countries: Kiss, Bow, or Shake Hands* (1994). Bob Adams, Holbrook MA. (Gives insights into 60 countries' negotiating/behavior styles.)

Scott Peck (1987). *The Different Drum: Community-Making and Peace*, Simon and Schuster, New York.

R. C. Wade, M.(Ed.) *Joining Hands: From Personal to Planetary Friendship in the Primary Classroom,* Zephyr Press, P.O. Box 13448, Tucson, AZ 85732-3448 (Grades PreK-3).

J. Zimmerman, *Council,* Atrium Publications, Box 1620 Ojai, CA 93023 1-850-640-0550.

D. Levin (1994). T*eaching Young Children In Violent Times: Building A Peaceable Classroom,* New Society Publishers, 4527 Springfield Ave., Phila., PA 19143 (PreK-3)

H. L. Floye, et.al. (1991).*Cooperative Learning in the Early Childhood Classroom,* NAEYC, Washington DC.

R. Devries and L. Kohlberg (Eds., 1987)."Moral Discussion and the Class Meeting," article by T. Lickona and L. Kohlberg, in *Constructivist Early Education: Overview and Comparison with Other Programs,* NAEYC, 1509 16th St NW, Washington, DC 20036.

For Children

L. Cherry, *The Great Kapok Tree*, World Almanac Education, PO Box 94556, Cleveland, OH 44101-4556.

B. Berger (1982/1994). *Animalia,* Tricycle Press, PO Box 7123, Berkeley, CA 94707.

K. Scholes, *Peace Begins With You*, Phila., PA Sierra Club Press. (Grades K-3).

J. Hissey (1990). *Jolly Tall: An Old Bear Story*. New York: Philomel Books, a division of Putman & Grosset. Story of a community of stuffed animals, and their discovery of a new friend. Illustrates caring, cooperation.

R. Isadora (1991). *At the Crossroads*. New York: Greenwillow. The community spirit, the love of the children, the cooperation and life-style, are beautifully portrayed.

N. Luenn (1993). *Song for the Ancient Forest*. New York: Macmillan. This story of Raven's struggle to save his land from logging and his communications people, is beautiful. A girl develops an ally in her father and they work together to save the forest. (Grades K-3).

C. Raschka (1993). *Yo! Yes?* New York: Orchard. Very few words tell a moving story about two boys of different races who become friends. It's an anti-bias reader and a story of friendship.

O. Kirkpatrick (1979). *Naja, the Snake and Mangus the Mongoose*, New York: Doubleday (Grades 1-3).

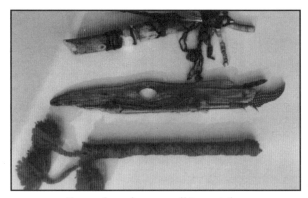

Examples of some talking sticks.

Building Community Through Empowerment and Guidelines

Introduction:

As mentioned, a starting point in building a community of peace with children is increasing their empowerment. Empowerment is integral to peace education, because when they know they have an impact, children are more likely to participate. The more they participate, the more inclusive the group's decisions become. When children feel included, they are more willing to engage in the process of co-creating a peacemaking classroom.

If children, or people of any age, perceive themselves as powerless, they are unlikely to make peaceful contributions to the community. Instead, they often respond with violence, acting out behaviors, or withdrawing. *Authoritarian messages* such as the following, can feel very oppressive to children:
1. "These are the rules, and you shall abide by them."
2. "This is my classroom, and I'll have none of that!"
3. "I don't care who started it, you both have to . . . "
4. "If you can't behave yourself, I'm going to have to call your mom."

These statements convey the message that the adult makes all the decisions and children are incapable of working out their conflicts with each other or with the teacher. Additionally, they eliminate the opportunity for children to practice their nonviolent conflict resolution skills.

Children also may have experienced *permissive messages:*
1. "Just be nice to each other."

2. "We don't hit or kick each other here, just play nicely."
3. "Let's not fight now, children."

These statements convey the message that conflict is to be avoided; there are no problems or conflicts in this happy classroom, and there is no further room for discussion. Children learn that in order to get along, we all need to agree. If we don't, we should hide our true feelings, and go along with the group. This can be tremendously frustrating to children, since their feelings are not being validated, and their conflicts are not being resolved.

Children are empowered when they have substantial opportunities to experience *freedom-within-limits messages* like:
1. "Let's make a decision together."
2. "Peace has been interrupted. What can we do about it?"
3. "Will you work this out with me?"
4. "In a peacemaking class we respect each other. What can you contribute to make this situation better?"
5. "Remember, one of the guidelines we all agreed to is . . . "
6. "Do you need to cool off, or are you ready to work this out now?"
7. "It looks like you want to ____. Let me show you a safe way to do this."

Many freedom-within-limits messages are questions. When adults model asking respectful questions and listening carefully to the responses, it's empowering to children, and gives the community the benefit of everyone's ideas.

Freedom Within Limits
Making Decisions Together

When problems or conflicts arise, the authoritarian approach is to take control of the situation and tell children what they must do or say, and what the punitive consequences will be if they refuse. The permissive response is not to mention the problem at all, or try to make the problem go away without addressing the feelings of the people involved or taking ownership of the problem.

The freedom-within-limits approach, sees the adult functioning as a gentle guide -- demonstrating and encouraging the children to think of more effective alternatives, and listening to their thoughts and feelings. Problems are owned, identified and respectfully resolved.

In this milieu, both adults and children define the limits. Guidelines for the classroom or the laws of the society, serve as the limits, within those limits are numerous opportunities for freedom of choice.

For example, a community guideline may state, "We take care of the classroom and the earth." The freedom for children within that guideline might be to decide what contributions they each want to make. For instance, children can decide how they want to help with the community cleanup when their individual work is put away. The class also can decide if it would like the structure of a job chart, prefers to choose to do these tasks on a daily volunteer basis, or intends to find some other solution.

When we invite a great deal of participation from the group, to determine the appropriate behaviors for our community, the children will reveal limits they feel are necessary for their well-being, and the guidelines will become relevant and important to them. We can listen for their self-imposed limits and help them learn how to frame them in a positive, rather than punishing, way. We also can thank them for their insights and contributions to the community. As a teacher, you can add limits you feel you need.

Barbara Coloroso, author of *Kid's Are Worth It,* reminds us to follow the Golden Rule in establishing limits with children. To paraphrase, she says, if we are not sure about something we are doing with the children, we can put ourselves in their place and ask if we would want it done to us? If the answer is "no," then we have to ask ourselves, "Why we are doing it to our children?"

Additional Reading:
B. Coloroso, *Kids Are Worth It: Giving Your Child the Gift of Inner Discipline* (1994). Willima Morrow, New York.
M. Shure, *Raising A Thinking Child* (1994). Henry Holt, New York.
Pyramid Film and Video *Why Do These Kids Love School,* (video) PO Box 1048, Santa Monica, CA 90406.
G. Wood, *Schools that Work: Anmerica's Most Innovative Public Education Programs*, ASCD, 1250 Pitt St. Alexandria, VA 22314-1453.

To Read With Children
R. Skutch, *Who's in A Family* (1995). Tricycle Press, PO Box 7123 Berkeley, CA 94707.

Characteristics of a Freedom-Within-Limits Classroom Community

1. Each student is a valued and an important member of the community . . . so much so that when one child is absent, he or she is missed. A moment of silence can be taken by the class to send caring, loving thoughts to this person and celebrate his/her return.
2. Everyone's feelings and ideas are important and respected when making decisions.
3. Routines are provided but become flexible when necessary.
4. Rules are established by the group.
5. Mistakes are viewed as an opportunity for growth and personal responsibility.
6. Conflict resolution skills are employed for staff/staff, staff/child and child/child disagreements.
7. Every child and teacher finds the opportunity to reach his or her highest potential with available resources.
8. Humor and laughter are commonplace.
9. Encouragement and support are mainstays as children try to master skills.
10. All feelings are O.K. Acting on feelings is done nonviolently.
11. Children are encouraged to share what they would like to learn.
12. Adults are emotionally available to the children.
13. Children are encouraged how to think rather than what to think.
14. Creativity is highly valued and celebrated.

I Can Make Peace All Over the Land
by Julie P. Peterson (children sing bold areas)

Chorus: **These are my feet these are my hands**
I can make peace all over the land.

With feet I walk. **With feet I walk**
I walk the peacemaker walk
With hands I work. **With hands I work**
I care, I share, and I talk 'cause (chorus)

With feet I walk. **With feet I walk**
My walk takes me through some tough choices
With hands I work. **With hands I work**
My hands do the work that my voice says (chorus)

With feet I walk. **With feet I walk**
I make lots of friends on my way
With hands I work. **With hands I work**
I want to hear everyone say (chorus)

With feet I walk. **With feet I walk**
I make friends from many countries
With hands I work. **With hands I work**
I know that's the way that it must be. (chorus)

Building Community Through Empowerment and Guidelines

Introduction:

As you involve the children in as much community decision-making as possible, an excellent place to start is by inviting them to develop the classroom rules or guidelines. Their involvement in this process will strengthen their commitment to the guidelines and build community. When children are empowered in this way they will begin to trust their voice will be heard and their opinions are highly valued. This increases the chances of children striving for cooperation and win-win solutions. It also reduces the frequency or necessity of intervention.

The following exercise will help children develop guidelines for a peaceful community. It's important that all the children agree to abide by the guidelines when completing this exercise.

The start of a new school year is a good time to introduce children to the idea of creating a community of peace. It's an opportunity for creating new guidelines, since the children may be expecting to learn new rules. However, if you are already beyond the beginning of the year, such a demarcation may not exist. Letting the children know that on a certain, special day, we will begin to make some peacemaking guidelines or rules together, is another successful approach to making these changes. We've chosen such dates as Martin Luther King Jr.'s birthday, the end of the winter holiday break, and Valentine's Day.

Goals:

1. To empower children in the decision-making process
2. To establish peaceful guidelines
3. To make a commitment to live by agreed upon guidelines
4. To create rituals for peacemaking gatherings and increase group bonding

Materials:

1. Drum
2. Poster-size paper
3. Markers
4. Talking stick

Presentation:

1. Invite children to community with a softly beating drum. We use 4/4 time with a simple 1,2,3,4. Emphasize the first beat. This rhythm promotes a peaceful gathering of the children. As you beat the drum, center yourself, and concentrate on your own inner peace. Breathe. Drumming will immediately set a peaceful tone for the group. Continue beating the drum until all the children have gathered at the circle taped on the floor. This activity eventually can be turned over to the children so they can take turns initiating the invitation to community. Continue meeting this way during each community time.

2. The teacher warmly greets the children and sings a *gathering* song of her/his/ choice. (Later, let the children choose gathering songs, and take turns leading the community.)

3. The teacher says something like, "Out of my love and concern for us, I would like to work together to find ways we can have a *peaceful classroom*. We often hear about people hurting each other or not caring about one another. I would like this to be place where we DO care about each other and we DO feel safe with each other. In our space, people are safe. Let's say this together." *In our space, people are safe.*

4. "In order to have a safe and peaceful classroom, what do you think we need for rules and guidelines for making peace. So we can hear from everyone, I'm going to pass the talking stick. Please share one idea you have for a *peaceful guideline* for our community. The rest of us will listen very carefully. I will write your idea on the paper. We'll keep doing this until everyone has had a chance to use the talking stick. This is the question I'd like to invite you to speak about: What is a rule or guideline you think we need to have, to have a peaceful and safe classroom?"

5. Label a piece of poster board, *Peace Agreement Chart*, and list the children's ideas. Be sure to state the guidelines in a positive manner such as, "Water the plants when they are dry," rather than, "Don't let the plants die," and "Respect each other's work," rather than, "Don't wreck each other's work." Some guidelines you might want to say when it is your turn, if they are not already stated are:
1. We listen to each other.
2. We show we care about others by respecting their work.
3. We are responsible for what we say and do.
4. We use respectful touch.

5. *We say "Please stop!" when someone is bothering us.*
6. *We stop when we are asked.*
7. *We take care of the classroom and the Earth.*

6. To focus on personal responsibility, go on to say, "Peace starts with each one of us. What each one of us does, as peacemakers, makes a difference to the other people in our classroom community, and to the people in our families. It makes a difference to the plants and animals. It makes a difference to the whole world. **I'm so excited, we are learning to be peacemakers!"**

7. Conclude with a peace signing ceremony for the *Peace Agreement Chart*. Explain, "Leaders of countries all over the world use their signature, or sign their name, to agreements or promises. If all of you feel we have a list of guidelines that we can live by, we can have a signing ceremony. Does anyone feels we need to make some changes?" *No.* "Since we all agree, we can have a signing ceremony! (Invite children to sign or mark.) We will put our Peace Agreement Chart on the wall, and, if we forget to follow a guideline, we can remind ourselves, or others can remind us, to keep our peace agreement." (Children can add or delete guidelines throughout the course of the year as needed and agreed to. Teachers can make a condensed list of 4 or 5 rules, for the community to memorize. Hang it in the classroom, and share it with families -- but be sure to keep the original list up!)

8. As a closing exercise, put the word *peace* on the chalkboard and do the following chant: Rhythm is 4/4
P-E-A-C-E, P-E-A-C-E, P-E-A-C-E
1, 2, 3, + 4   1, 2, 3,+ 4   1, 2, 3, + 4
Peace, Peace, Peace.
1   2   3 (4).

Empowerment of the Children:
1. Deciding together what rules or guidelines are needed in order to have a peaceful classroom
2. Signing the peace agreement
3. Talking without being interrupted
4. Realizing everyone's ideas are valued

Points of Interest:
1. Listening to the drumming
2. Seeing the teacher concentrating on his or her inner peace
3. Being asked for ideas
4. Seeing ideas being recorded in print
5. Having a signing ceremony
6. Hearing and seeing what guidelines help make a peacemaking environment
7. Using a talking stick while speaking

Language Development:
1. Peace Agreement
2. Peaceful classroom
3. Guidelines
4. Signing ceremony
5. Spelling "Peace"
6. Gathering
7. Closing ceremony
8. Peacemaker

Extensions and Variations:
1. **Ask the children to name their community.** They can come up with anything they like that is respectful and is related to peace. If the entire school embraces this idea, you can have a central theme and each class can use a name that reflects that theme. For instance, if *peace* is the theme, each class can be a different peace symbol: dove, rainbow, cloud, sun, butterfly, tree, and so on. Ask the administration to refer to each class by it's community name. Instead of "Mrs. Black's Class" it might be the Rainbow Community, or the Cloud Community!

2. **Make up a community chant** for use at community gathering times. It's nice if it can be responsive. The child in charge of the gathering, or the teacher, says the community name, like: "Rainbow community." The others answer "Yes!" (with lots of energy). Then the leader might say, "Unity." The others answer, "Yes!" And finally, the leader might say, "Peace." The others say, "Yes!" The possibilities are unlimited. This tradition has its roots in African culture, if you wish to research it further.

3. **Children can draw a picture of themselves, on a page of their peace journal,** *doing* **one of the guidelines on the peace agreement.** For example, they might want to draw themselves taking care of the classroom by putting their work away, or watering the plants, or walking instead of running in the classroom, or using the talking stick, and so on.

4. **Children can take one of the guidelines and demonstrate it** in words, in music, in dance, in sculpture, in graphs, reports, in an interview, with a puppet, on a bulletin board, in clay, in a play, in any way that helps them show or demonstrate the guideline. This helps them internalize and better understand and implement the guidelines.

5. **Cooperative pairs or small groups can demonstrate** a guideline in a role play or with puppets.

6. **Older children can copy the guidelines** in their peace journals or copy them to take home and show their family.

7. **Children can work in cooperative pairs and color** a border around the peace agreement.

8. **Read *John, John Twilliger* by** William Wondriska (1966). Holt,

Rinehart and Winston (Grade PreK-4). A simple story of a young boy and his dog transforming and disarming a town tyrant by teaching him to dance and enjoy life. Useful for teaching about dictatorship and that people do not need to put up with irrational and repressive rules. Can be borrowed from the Philadelphia Yearly Meeting Library, 1515 Cherry St. Phila., PA 19102 (341.19JF W).

Teaching Tips:
1. When a guideline is broken during the first six weeks of school or a child's first six weeks in your classroom, a gentle reminder of what the Peace Agreement entails is all that is necessary to make sure the child understands. Remind the child in a positive and personal way by walking over and:
a. Stating the guideline ("Remember, we put our work back on the shelf when it is cleanup time.)
b. Stating the reason for the guideline ("Each one of us is responsible for clean up, because we agreed or promised to make the classroom ready and beautiful for the next time we work together.")
c. Offering a choice if possible ("Do you want to put this away first, or that away first?")

2. Involve parents with your guideline process by sending home a letter like this:

Dear Parent(s)
Our class has developed a set of peacemaking rules which we have all agreed to follow throughout the year. We invite you to be our partners in the goal of having a peaceful classroom. Please save these rules and ask your child to explain them to you.

Throughout the year we'll be doing other activities for Peace. We are learning that peace starts with each individual and that it's important for all of us to take responsibility for our actions. If you have any questions about our peacemaking skills lessons, I would be happy to chat with you.

Thanks very much,
(Send home with a copy of the *Peaceful Agreement Chart*.)

3. Role Play: Children can be taught how to interrupt others, including the teacher, in a nonverbal, peaceful, respectful way. During community time demonstrate "How to Interrupt Someone Peacefully." Ask for two volunteers to do a role play with you. Pretend you are sitting working with the first child and another child wants your attention. When he or she comes over to you, show how to interrupt you by putting his or her hand on your shoulder and tapping it lightly one time. Acknowledge the child by turning your head and nodding or smiling. This reassures the child that you will attend to his or her needs when you are finished working with his/her classmate. If you are standing, the child can touch your hand and you turn and nod. In addition to building a trusting, caring and respectful relationship with the children, you will experience interruptions in a more peaceful way! You may want to repeat this role play with more than one child. Children can interrupt each other when working by saying, "May I please work with you?" or "May I please watch you?" (See Communication Skills Lessons.)

Other Ideas for Building Community Through Empowerment

Rename: "Show and Tell" as "Public Speaking" Not only is this a time for children to share with the group their peacemaking thoughts or experiences with their community, but it gives children individual practice in speaking before others. Choosing a starter sentence when no one spontaneously offers to speak can be helpful:
1. Something [peaceful] I did with my family . . .
2. Something [peaceful] I experienced in nature . . .
3. A peacemaking idea I have . .
4. A peacemaker I know is . . .

Public speaking is a common fear, but we have found, over a period of time, children begin to say, "I need to do public speaking," when they have something to share. If the children insist on talking about material possessions, and celebrating violent toys or television programs, your thoughtful questions such as, "What else can that be used for?" or "Can you think of a nonviolent way they could have solved that problem?" will stimulate their creativity and enhance their ability to see and experience peace. This public forum empowers children (at a later time) to have a history of speaking up about topics or issues pertinent to their lives, which may be threatening peace. It also empowers them to serve as leaders in creating peaceful communities.

Teach children about silence.
Children need opportunities to

practice and experience quiet as a valued behavior. They can enhance their sense of gratitude as they learn to listen more deeply to the sounds of the Earth, and they can learn to celebrate quiet time as valued reflection time for themselves.

Many have learned to interpret "BE QUIET!" as "I've done something I shouldn't have done," or "I'm being punished." Thus, "quiet" has negative connotations for them. Children can practice making silence, like they practice other activities. A fun activity to experience quiet as a joyful experience during community time, is rainmaking. It starts as a small shower, turns into a big rainstorm, and eventually fades out again.

Rainmaking Exercise:
Stand in a circle. Children copy the teacher who stands in the center. The teacher says, "When I look at you, start doing exactly what I'm doing with my hands or feet. Don't start the action until I look right at you, and don't stop doing that until I look at you again and show you something else to do. But when I sit down, you all sit down very quietly with me." Look at each child one at a time and begin rubbing hands together until you have completed the circle. "Listen carefully, so you can hear the sound of yourself and the others. Our sounds are going to work together to make something special!" Then switch the children from rubbing hands to snapping fingers or tapping fingers together the same way you did for rubbing hands. (They continue doing the motion until you look at them again and give them a new motion. Thus, some are still

rubbing hands together, while others have begun to tap. With very young children, you can do the motions all together rather than as a round.) After this, go around with clapping, then stamping, and then stamping and patting thighs. When you have a very loud rainstorm, begin to decrease the rainstorm by reversing the order until you are all very quietly rubbing hands together. Finally, motion the children to silence their hands and then very quietly sit down. Practice silence together for a few moments with relaxed breathing. Ask the children to close their eyes and listen to their own breathing. This can become a silence-making game the children want to repeat many times throughout the year.

Later on, you can move into relaxation exercises such as asking them to imagine they are in a field of beautiful flowers, or near a smooth lake or invite them to tense and relax different parts of their bodies. If they are wiggling, they will get better at it. Just do a tiny bit at each sitting, gradually increasing the relaxation exercise and the length of silent time.

Additional Reading
P. Greenberg (July, 1992). "Ideas That Work With Young Children. How to Institute Some Simple Democratic Practices Pertaining to Respect, Rights, Roots and Responsibility in Any Classroom (Without Losing Your Control)" *Young Children* 47, No. 5, NAEYC.

J. Hendrick (March, 1992). "Where Does It All Begin? Teaching the Principles of Democracy in the Early Years," *Young Children* 47, No. 3, NAEYC.

K. McGinnis and B. Oehlberg (1988). *Starting Out Right: Nurturing Young Children As Peacemakers.* Oak Park, IL: Meyer Stone Books.

D. Johnson and R. Johnson (1991). *Teaching Students to Be Peacemakers.* Edina, MN: Interaction Book Company.

C. Cherry (1981). *Think of Something Quiet: A Guide For Achieving Serenity In Early Childhood Classrooms,* Pitman Learning, Inc., 6 Davis Drive, Belmont, California 94002. (Grades PreK).

E. McGinnis and A. Goldstein (1990). *Skill Streaming in Early Childhood: Teaching Prosocial Skills to the Preschool and Kindergarten Child,* Research Pr., Champaign, IL.

N. Schniendewind, and E. Davidson, *Cooperative Learning, Cooperative Lives: A Sourcebook of Learning Activities for Building A Peaceful World* (Grades 1-6).

C. Anderson (Ed. 1993) *Rings of Empowerment: A Guide to Discovering and Fulfilling Your Life Purpose as Part of a Co-creative Team,* Global Family, 112 Jordan Ave. San Anselmo, CA

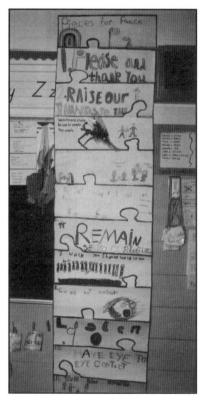

"Pieces for Peace," classroom guidelines poster in a second grade classroom community.

Building Community Through Understanding Conflict
Understanding Conflict Lesson

Conflict Isn't Bad!?

Child 1: "In our class, we're learning that conflict isn't bad."
Child 2: "Come on, your teacher is not telling you the truth! When I see people in conflict, it's awful!"
Child 1: "That's just because they don't know how to work out their conflict, and learn from it."
Child 2: "Really? Learn in a conflict? What do you mean?"

Introduction:

The Chinese symbol for crisis also is the symbol for opportunity. Many of us do not view crisis as an opportunity. In fact, when a crisis is a conflict, many of us have learned to avoid it, or try to put an immediate end to it. This attitude can substantially hurt our ability to learn from each other. In fact, D. W. Johnson and R. T. Johnson, whose specialty is cooperative learning, write extensively on this topic. They point out that while we can not accept or condone *violence*, there are some definite benefits to *conflict*. Conflicts can

1. increase achievement;
2. increase motivation to learn;
3. increase higher-level reasoning;
4. increase long-term retention;
5. increase healthy social development;
6. increase ego strength;
7. increase the fun students have in school;
8. enrich relationships;
9. clarify personal identity;
10. promote resilience in adversity;
11. clarify how one needs to change.

They go on to say, "It is not the presence of conflict that is to be feared but rather, its destructive management. Attempts to deny, suppress, repress, and ignore conflicts may, in fact, be a major contributor to the occurrence of violence in schools. Given the many positive outcomes of conflict, schools need to teach students how to manage conflicts constructively."[1]

Goals:

1. To define conflict
2. To reinforce the right to feel feelings during a conflict
3. To introduce nonviolence as a way to solve a conflict
4. To provide a healthy way to express anger through the journaling process
5. To understand nonviolence is a choice even when we are angry
6. To establish peace as the standard. It can be interrupted
7. To be able to act peacefully when reminding each other about the peace agreement

Materials:

1. Two puppets (teacher's choice "Sarah" a female puppet and "Jamie" a male)
2. Four children's blocks
3. Peace journals for each child
4. Crayons or water soluble markers
5. *I'm Mad* song on *We Can Solve it Peacefully* audiotape
6. Drum

Presentation:

1. Invite the children to community with the drum. After they are seated, walk around the inside of the circle and greet each child by shaking her/his hand and saying, "Hi, Peacemaker _____ (child's name). Hi, Peacemaker _____ (child's name). Congratulations on making the 'Peace Agreement' chart! We have some wonderful guidelines to help us be peacemakers. Let's say them together." (Younger children can repeat after you.) "That was fun!

2. "Remember, if someone forgets one of the guidelines, we can remind each other by saying, 'Remember the peace agreement guidelines?' or 'Do you need some help?'

3. "Sometimes *peace can be interrupted* because two people want the same thing at the same time. Sometimes peace can be interrupted because people have different ideas about how something might be used. There are many ways peace can be interrupted. When peace is interrupted it is sometimes called a *conflict*. Let's say that together." *Conflict*.

4. "Let's watch what happens to these puppets when peace is interrupted. I'll do a *puppet play* with them."

5. Show puppets Sarah and Jamie playing with four blocks. "They are playing peacefully." Next, have Sarah take all the blocks and say, "I'm going to build a tower. I need all the blocks. You can't have any." Jamie tries to take some of the blocks back. Sarah pushes Jamie and says, "No! I need all the blocks. I got this work out and I'm the boss." She pushes Jamie away.

[1] D.W. Johnson, and R.T. Johnson, "Why Violence Prevention Programs Don't Work -- and What Does" (Feb., 1995). *Educational Leadership*, 52:5 p. 64.

Jamie is angry and says, "I'm telling!" and pushes Sarah.

6. Stop the puppet play and say, "Peace got interrupted. They are having a *conflict* or problem. *They have different ideas about how the blocks should be used.* It's O.K. to have different ideas but it is not O.K. to be *violent* and push each other because of *differences*.

7. "Both Sarah and Jamie are *mad* or *angry*. It's also O.K. to feel mad, but it is not O.K. to be violent when we're feeling mad.

8. "Let's listen to a song called, *I'm Mad,* and find out what happens when some other peace-makers are feeling mad or *angry*." (Play the *I'm Mad* song.)

9. "Peacemakers do get angry sometimes, but it's no reason to start hitting each other. Did you hear the word *Peacemaker*ˢᴹ in that song? She is my friend. She made this audiotape so we can learn how to solve our conflicts peacefully. In a few days she'll be here to visit us! She believes each one of us has the power to be a peacemaker if we learn about peace and practice being a peacemaker every day. She told me she will help us learn *nonviolent* behaviors, so we can choose an *alternative to violence* if peace gets interrupted in our community.

Peacemakers choose nonviolence even when they're angry. Let's say that together with power in our voices." *Peacemakers choose nonviolence even when they're angry.* "One more time!" *Peacemakers choose nonviolence even when they're angry.*

10. Hand out the peace journals. "To get ready for *Peacemaker'sˢᴹ*

visit, let's draw a picture in our peace journals of a conflict or problem we have had when we were feeling *so* mad." (For non-writers, record their descriptions under their drawing. Writers can record their own description.) Play the *I'm Mad* song again if time allows.

11. Close with the PEACE chant.

Empowerment of the Children:
1. Everyone has a right to their feelings
2. When inappropriate behaviors happen, peace has been interrupted and can be handled nonviolently
3. Children remind each other to be peacemakers
4. Children offer to help each other

Points of Interest:
1. Seeing a puppet play
2. Drawing in the peace journal
3. Having an adult listen and record thoughts
4. Listening to how other children feel about conflict on the *I'm Mad* song

Language Development:
1. Puppet play
2. Conflict
3. Angry/mad
4. Differences/different ideas
5. Peace can be *interrupted*
6. *Peacemakerˢᴹ* (as a unique character as well as who they are).
7. Violence
8. Nonviolence
9. Alternative to violence

Extensions and Variations:
1. **Children share oral stories** about previous conflicts in their lives using the talking stick.

2. **Children draw** more than one picture in the peace journal.
3. **Children define the problem** two characters are having in a storybook or TV show they remember.
4. **Children share what they know** about world conflicts.
5. **Practice *I'm Mad* song.** Encourage children to learn the words and sing along.
6. **An alternative to violence is cooperation.** Try creating a cooperative rainbow. Make an outline of a rainbow in several sections with several different colors of large paper adjoining each other. Each child paints his or her hand and makes hand prints between the drawn lines on the paper. The pieces can be cut out and pinned or taped to the wall or bulletin board. The finished product will look like a rainbow of hands. This makes a great visual display for the children to remind them they are a community of peacemakers.
7. Each child decorates a strip of construction paper to represent one person in the community. Strips can be stapled together to

---

How Could Anyone

*How could anyone ever tell you
You were anything less than beautiful?
How could anyone ever tell you,
You were less than whole?
How could anyone fail to notice,
That your loving is a miracle?
How deeply you're connected to my soul.*

Libby Rodderick[1]

---

[1] Words and music by Libby Roderick © 1988 Libby Roderick Music. From the recording, If You See A Dream, Turtle Island Records, P.O. Box 203294, Anchorage, Alaska 99520 (907) 278-6817 (Used with permission. Highly recommended)

make a chain of peacemakers. Children are invited to hold the peacemaker chain and move in a circle singing, *The More We Get Together.*

The more we get together, together, together, The more we get together, the happier we'll be, 'Cause your friends are my friends, And my friends are your friends, The more we get together, the happier we'll be.[1]

[1] Recorded by Raffi (1976) *Singable Songs for the Very Young*, Troubadour Records.

Additional Reading
E.Crary (1984). *Kids Can Cooperate* Parenting Press, Inc.
S. Wichert, *Keeping the Peace: Practicing Cooperation and Conflict Resolution with Preschoolers*
S. Judson (1984). *A Manual on Nonviolence and Children*, New Society, Phila. PA.
A. Parry (September, 1993). "Children Surviving in a Violent World -- Choosing Non-Violence." *Young Children* 48, No. 6 pp.13-15.

To Read With Children
R. Erickson (1974). *A Toad for Tuesday*, Lothrop.
B. Peck, *Mathew and Tilly*, Dutton Children's Books.
J. Oppenheim, *On the Other Side of the River*, Franklin Watts.
T. dePaola (1980). *The Knight and the Dragon* New York: G.P. Putnam.
A. Broomall, ed. (1949/1990). *The Friendly Story Caravan*, Wallingford, PA, Pendle Hill Publications.
C. Lohn (1983). *The Sun and the Wind*, Newton KS: Faith and Life Press.
A. Lobel (1982). *Ming Lo Moves the Mountain*. New York: Greenwillow.
W. Kriodler (1994). *Teaching Conflict Resolution Through Children's Literature*. Scholastic. 555 Broadway, New York, NY 10012.

Building A Community of Peacemakers Through Communication Skills

Introduction:

Throughout our lives we will continue to have conflicts. When young children have the opportunity to try to solve problems nonviolently throughout their childhood, they will have a long history of practice as problem solvers when they enter adulthood. With this history and skill development, they will be more likely to believe that problems can be resolved nonviolently, and act accordingly. Since skill development and knowledge of choices is directly related to the ability to solve problems nonviolently, it is our responsibility to expose children to effective conflict resolution skills at each developmental stage of their lives.

When peace gets interrupted, we may have an emerging conflict, or a full-blown conflict. In a full-blown conflict we can use the A,B,Cs of conflict resolution described in Chapter IV. However, with emerging, or small conflicts, a formal conflict resolution process may not be necessary. Some simple verbal statements can restore harmony quickly and easily.

"Please Stop!" Statements
The ability to say, "Please stop!" is a very important beginning step to personal power, and holds both children involved, accountable. If a child reports an incident, the teacher can say, "Did you say, 'Please stop?'" If the answer is "no," the child can be invited to go back and do that (if no physical violence was involved). The

teacher can stand by, and give support if necessary. If the child did say, "Please stop!" originally, and the other child didn't stop, that child might be ready to stop now, since you have been summoned. If necessary, remind the other child that in our guidelines we agreed to stop when someone says, "Please stop." If the child still chooses not to stop, he or she is very likely having some difficulty at the moment and may need a cooling off period or can be invited to share that difficulty and more clearly define the problem.

This verbal statement encourages the first child to identify and communicate his or her boundaries or preferences in an assertive but not threatening manner. The other child receives a very clear message and has the opportunity to choose to change his or her behavior. Often this simple procedure is enough for children to redirect their own behavior and exhibit self-discipline and cooperation.

"May I Please Play With You?"
When a child wants to join in with another's play or work, a request that prevents many conflicts is, "May I please work (or play) with you?" "May I please watch you?" is another appropriate request.

"What Can I Do to Show I'm Sorry?"
A useful statement to use when

someone has been hurt is to ask the child who did the hurtful behavior to say, "What can I do to show I'm sorry?" rather than "I'm sorry." This is more effective because it holds the child accountable and affords an opportunity to make amends. The hurt child is more able to move away from resentment and anger by stating his or her needs, and by receiving help for the current problem. Both children are able to reconnect instead of suffer a strained relationship or become temporary enemies. The child who did the hurtful behavior has the opportunity to see himself or herself as being capable of being a loving and caring person. For example, the child might be able to hold an ice bag on a slightly injured child's head.

Compassionate Assertiveness

There are many ways to use assertive statements to express our feelings. We find being *both* assertive and caring in a single statement is an effective way for children to let another person know their feelings and the specific behavior they would like to have happen. This can stop many conflicts in the early stages.

Compassionate assertiveness often begins as a "Please stop!" state-ment, but continues as a compas-sionate connecting statement. It is a way a child can say "no" or "stop" and also be affirming of the other child.

For example: Jamal is playing with some blocks. Judith comes over and starts playing with the same blocks. Jamal might say: "Please stop! Go away!" If Jamal stops there, Judith might leave his work alone, but may feel alienated or hurt. When Judith feels rejected or thinks she is being left

out, she is less likely to improve her behavior. In fact, the disrup-tive behavior may escalate.

If Jamal begins in the same way: "Please stop!" and continues with a compassionate statement like: "I want to work alone right now, *but I'll play with you in a little while,"* Judith knows she isn't being rejected as a person. Thus, children are able to prevent many emerging conflicts from escalating. Children who express themselves like this are letting the other person know their boundaries (being assertive), in a caring manner (compassionately). Examples of compassionate assertiveness are included in the second session below.

Communication Skills Lessons:

Goals:
1. To demonstrate assertive language skills
2. To increase understanding that peacemakers stop when asked
3. To announce it's O.K. to use assertive statements first, instead of tattling
4. To confirm it's O.K. to set boundaries and communicate them
5. To build self esteem
6. To show we bring peace to others when we smile

Materials:
1. Two puppets of your choice (Sarah and Jamie)
2. Some favorite blocks or toys
3. *I Smile at Myself* song from *We Can Solve it Peacefully* audiotape
4. Ball of yarn or rope

Presentation:

1. Invite one of the children to gather the community with the sound of a softly beating drum.

2. Greet the children and say, "I am so glad we are learning to be peacemakers!

3. "Today we'll learn how peace-makers tell each other, in a respectful way, when peace has been interrupted. We don't use hitting, kicking, biting, yelling, ignoring each other, name calling, or teasing. A peacemaker can see that peace has been interrupted, and will work out a problem with no violence.

4. "Sometimes, as peacemakers we practice what they are going to do when there is a problem, before we even have the problem. There will be time today to practice some of our skills.

5. "Peacemakers know how to say, 'Please stop!' when someone is bothering us. We peacemakers *will* stop doing what we are doing when asked. We stop because we are being respectful and this is a classsroom where we care about each other."

6. The scenarios for your puppet plays might be:
1. One puppet is saying something hurtful to the other.
2. One puppet is hitting.
3. One puppet wrecks another's work.
4. One puppet joins the other's work area without asking.

Choose a scenario (from the above list), and a corresponding "Please stop!" statement (from the follow-ing list), and do a puppet play. Example 3 is played out for you:

Example 1: "Please stop! That hurts my feelings."

Example 2: "Please stop! That hurts my body."

Example 3: "Please stop! I want you to respect my work."

Example 4: "Please stop! I want to play alone right now."

Directions for the puppet play using Example 3: "Let's pretend one puppet *interrupts* peace by pushing over the tower of blocks the other is building." (Demonstrate with puppets.) "The puppet whose blocks have been pushed over says, **'Please stop! I want you to respect my work,'** and the other puppet stops and says, 'O.K.'" (Demonstrate with puppets.) "The puppet who interrupted peace goes on to play or work with someone else. The other puppet says, *'Thank you for caring about me.'"*

7. Continue to demonstrate with these scenarios (or others) and the "Please Stop!" statements with the puppets, and/or try them as role plays with the children.

Second Session
"May I Please?" and
Compassionate Assertiveness

1. "Now that we know how to say 'Please stop!' let's learn some other words that can help us. If you want to play with someone, that person will be more likely to invite you if you ask politely, instead of pushing or shoving to join in. You can ask, 'May I please work (or play) with you?' and then respect the answer you get. Let's watch the puppets do this." (Do this simple role play with the second puppet saying, "Yes, you may work with me." Practice as a group with the children repeating after you, "May I please work with you?")

2. "If someone wants to play with you, but you don't want to play with that person right now, you can say, 'No thank you, but thanks for asking.' You can give that person a smile, too." Demonstrate with puppets as in #1, but have the second puppet turn down the request.

3. "Sometimes our feelings are hurt if someone says 'no' to us. But peacemakers say 'no' sometimes. Since we want to be gentle with each other's feelings, let's learn a peaceful way to say 'no.' It's called *compassionate assertiveness*, two big words that mean saying 'no' kindly. The puppets will show us how to do it."

4. Puppet play: One puppet asks to play with the other. The puppet being asked says, "No, but you can get your things and work next to me." The asking puppet acts happy, not rejected. Invite the children to role play a few examples from the list below. The scenarios are implied. You can make this more relevant to the children, by using scenarios you have seen in the community (also see **Teaching Tip** below):

Example 1: "Please stop playing with my toys! I want to play alone, *but get your toys and sit next to me."*

Example 2: "Please stop hurting Gilly! She is my favorite doll. *Please use her nicely. We can play with her together."*

Example 3: "Please stop asking me to play! I feel tired right now, *but I still like you."*

Example 4: "I want to work alone right now, *but I'll play with you in a little while."*

Third Session
Interconnectedness

1. "Another way of showing we care about each other's feelings is by smiling at each other. Let's practice smiling at each other by playing the smiling game with this ball of yarn. I'll start by holding a piece of the yarn, and passing the ball to Jerad. When he has it, I'll give him a smile. Jerad, you hold a piece of the yarn, and pass it to someone across the circle from you, who hasn't had the yarn ball yet. Be sure to give that person a big smile!"

2. Continue until all the children are connected. Keep the yarn taut.

3. "We are all connected to each other every minute, not just right now, with the yarn. This yarn helps us see and feel what happens when one person in our community shares a smile or a kind thought. Shut your eyes, and hold your piece of yarn very carefully."

4. Pluck on the web. "Can you feel that? Yes, we can feel it, because we are all connected. Now open your eyes to see how I did that." (Pluck a strand again.) "I would like to invite each one of you to say a kind thought about yourself, and pluck the web after you say it. We can feel kindness. Kindness to ourselves, and to others, is very powerful." (Go around the circle.)

5. "Now I need cooperation to roll up this web. I would like to try an idea I have for getting the yarn back into a ball. Pass a smile back to the person who gave us the yarn ball, toss the yarn back to that person, and we'll roll up the yarn and cooperate!"

6. When the children are taking turns rolling up the yarn web, play the *I Smile at Myself* song.

Teaching Tip:
Teach other caring messages that might diffuse potential conflicts with your particular group of children. Here are some suggestions:
1. "I'll play with you later."
2. "I don't feel like doing that now, but that doesn't mean I don't like you. I might feel like doing that tomorrow."
3. "I am playing with Jessica right now, but you may join us."
4. "I like to use the computer by myself, but when I'm done, I will build something with you."

Empowerment of the Children:
1. Learning to use words to stop behavior they don 't like
2. Identifying their own bound-aries
3. Showing self control
4. Viewing themselves as peace-makers
5. Learning they are all connected to each other
6. Finding friendship in a smile

Points of Interest:
1. Puppet plays
2. Role plays
3. Teacher's sharing her/his happiness about learning peacemaking skills
4. Passing web of yarn and smiling
5. *I Smile at Myself* song

Language Development:
1. "Please Stop!"
2. "May I please work with you?"
3. Compassionate assertiveness statements.
4. "No thank you"
5. Connected
6. Smile
7. Kindness

Extensions and Variations:
1. **Children play the web game with the yarn**, and pluck the string to illustrate having a conflict. This demonstrates that conflicts impact others, just like smiles do. If the yarn gets tangled, say, "Look how tangled this web can get. Some problems are just like this -- they are hard to untangle! Sometimes it takes a long time."
2. **Sing the following words to tune of** *If You're Happy and You Know It*
   If you're peaceful and you know it, give a smile (repeat)
   If you're peaceful and you know it,
   Then you can really glow it,
   If you're peaceful and you know it, give a smile.

Additional Reading:
S. Berman (1983). *Perspectives: A Teaching Guide to Concepts of Peace*, Educators for Social Responsibility, 1490 Riverside Dr. Room 27, New York, NY 10027.
D. Dixon, *Teaching Children to Care: 80 Circle Time Activities for Primary Grades,* Twenty-Third publications, PO Box 180, 185 Willow St., Mystic, CT 06355.
Ed. Brody, Goldspinner, Green, Leventhal, and Porcino, *Spinning Tales Weaving Hope: Storytelling and Activities for Peace, Justice and the Environment* (1993). Zephyr Press, 3316 N. Chapel Ave., PO Box 66006-B, Tucson, AZ 85728.

I Smile

I look in the mirror, I see my own face.
It's the reflection of every race.
I know peace begins here, it begins within.
To celebrate all life I give me a grin.

I smile, I smile, smile at myself
Smile, smile, smile at myself
Smile, smile, smile at myself
And I watch my world change.
(Last time: And I fill my world with love.)

I'm never too little to make peace and give
It's a big job, it's my job as long as I live
For some it comes harder, I think that is me,
But I'm doing much better, I'm starting to see

That a smile at my own self is a good place to start
This journey toward peace must start in my heart
When I don't like myself much, it's hard to be kind
So I give me a big smile, and find peace of mind.

Peace Table Song

I want my way, you want yours
Oh what can we do?
I feel my way, you feel yours,
I want to work this out with you.

Chorus:
We're marching over to the peace table,
Marching over and we're very able
Marching over to the peace table.
Let's work it out right now.

A is always stop right now,
Ask to work it out somehow.
Say the problem, tell your part
Share the feelings in your heart.

B is brainstorm things to do
C is choose a plan to do
D is do it, then it's E
Evaluate with you and me.

F's for fairness for everyone,
Sharing all beneath the sun.
Can freedom and equality
Be everyone's reality?

Now we've solved it peacefully,
We are peacemaking now you see,
We've stopped our fight and worked it through,
Hooray, hooray! for me and you.

Alternatives to violence for age 6 and up.

Dear Children:

Congratulations on deciding to be peacemakers! Many children write to me with their questions. One of the most common questions is: "How do I handle teasing?"

Now that you know there are alternatives to violence, here are some ideas that you might want to try. If you come up with some other alternatives that work for you, please write them down and send them to me. I would like to learn them! Peacemakers are always trying to learn more alternatives to violence.

If you have a problem with someone teasing you, choose an idea to try. Try it consistently, and then evaluate its success. If you are unhappy with your results, try another approach, or get some help from a trusted friend or adult.

First decide if the person teasing you is going to physically hurt you. Most teasing is not physically dangerous. If you think it is, get an adult, tell your story, then ask to have help to work it out with the person.

Most often, teasers are trying to hurt someone's feelings. They might be trying to look big or important, or tough, or like a television hero. Maybe there is a big brother or sister, parent or other person in their lives who is hurting or teasing them. Teasing may be the way some people in their lives show they care about them. They might think teasing is O.K.

When someone teases me, the first thing I try is giving them a compliment! If someone says, "Gee you look awful today," I might say, "I really like your sweater," or "You really look nice today." This is so surprising to them sometimes they stop teasing right away! They might really need a compliment, and now that they got one -- a sincere one -- they might stop teasing. If I'm angry or scared, I tell myself it's O.K. to feel angry or scared, but I won't let it cause me to act in a violent or disrespectful way. I keep my body under control.

If I want to solve the problem peacefully or nonviolently, I state the problem in a respectful way, such as, "This person and I aren't getting along," or "We seem to have different ideas about . . ."

Another question I sometimes ask myself is, "Does this person really want to be friends, but feels left out by me and my friends? Does this person feel like an outsider? What would happen if I were more friendly and invited this person to play with me?

I also think about how much power I give away to someone who is teasing me or calling me names. If someone said, "You are a stop sign," I would think, "No, I'm not." So why should I believe it when someone calls me "dumb," or "stupid," unless I already believe it about myself? The bully has either reminded me of something I believe about myself already, or the bully isn't telling the truth. If the bully isn't telling the truth I'm just not going to get upset about it! I may even find it funny because it's so ridiculous! If it is something that is true about me, I might use one of these:

"Yeah, I may not be very good at doing this, but what I'm really good at is ____."
"Yeah, I may not be very good at doing this, do you know of anyone who can help me learn how to do it better?"
"Yeah, I know that is something that is true about me, but that's O.K. because it's not important to me right now."
"Please stop saying that to me. It hurts my feelings. If you are having a problem with me, I'll try to work it out with you. We don't need to be mean to each other just because we have a problem." (If I'm in a peacemaking classroom or home, and we know the process for working out our problems at a peace table, then I feel even more safe, knowing that if my other ideas don't work, I will still have another way to get my problem worked out peacefully.)

One of the great peacemakers of all time, Mohandus Gandhi, said being fearless is one of the most important virtues a peacemaker can have. Does this mean being fearless enough to punch someone? No. This means being fearless or brave enough to try to make peace -- even with a bully or an enemy. Sometimes it takes great courage to spend a few minutes with a bully, but this kind of courage can have peacemaking results.

Peace,

Peacemaker

Peacemaker

PS. The author Terrence Webster-Doyle has some good books that helped me with this subject. Children in kindergarten and up can begin to practice some of the things he suggests. *Facing the Double Edged Sword* (Atrium Publications, Ojai, CA, 1988), is very helpful for children and adults to get some ideas about dealing with bullies nonviolently.

CHAPTER IV LESSONS FOR THE MIDDLE OF THE PYRAMID: A Formal Conflict Resolution Process

Introduction:

Since children are concrete learners, they appreciate having a specific place designated for problem solving or conflict resolution. The peace table is in that space, which becomes a respected and appreciated area representing empowerment, not punishment.

The peace table is used exclusively for resolving conflicts so it is always available to the children when needed. A peace table helps the children feel they are in a safe and secure environment because they know they will have an opportunity to work out their problems, and their voice will be heard. Once the skills have been mastered at the peace table, other objects can serve as a peace table when outside or in places where there is no peace table available.

By beginning with this concrete object to anchor the concepts in reality, and to remind the children of *Peacemaker's A,B,Cs*, they eventually will learn a well-defined process for working out problems, and will be able to use the process anywhere -- often without adult assistance.

It is helpful to place the table and two chairs near a wall where *Peacemaker's A,B,Cs of Conflict Resolution*^{TM} (Chart) can be posted as a reference. Substitutes and parents also will be able to understand the problem solving process that the children are familiar with, and continue this work in your absence, or at home.

Peace Table:

Conflict partners sit at the peace table. Initially, the adult should assist the children until they learn all the steps.

With a peace table process available, children begin to realize it is their words and their willingness to work it out that resolves conflicts, not force or withdrawn behaviors.

Overview of the A,B,Cs of Conflict Resolution

A

It may be necessary for one or both of the children to have a "cooling off" period before coming to the peace table. This step, the first part of **A,** *Always stop right now*, is essential, and often is the only step necessary for children to resume playing or working together. The children determine when their "cooling off" period is over.

They may be ready to resume playing, or they can go on to the second part of A, *Ask to work it out somehow.* At that point, one asks the other to work it out.

B

The next step is B. As in step A, step B has two parts: *Become Communicators* and *Brainstorm*. Become communicators means using effective communication techniques, specifically I-messages, to take responsibility for, and express one's feelings nonviolently to the conflict partner. It also includes

active listening, where the listener restates the other person's feelings.

When conflict partners state their feelings and do active listening, they can begin to develop empathy and avoid a war with words.

Next, the children move to the second part of **B**, and *Brainstorm solutions* to the problem. The adult helps the children keep track of their ideas by writing them down or helping them to remember them when it is time to choose one.

C

The list of options is reviewed and the children *Choose* one they would like to try together. Consequences of each choice are considered. Consensus decision-making is critical.

D

Before leaving the table to *Do* their selected solution, they shake hands and say, "Thanks for working this out with me." The adult checks with the children later to. . .

E

. . . *Evaluate* the solution. If the children are pleased, he/she congratulates them. If the solution didn't work out, he/she suggests they come back to the peace table to find a different solution (If it doesn't work out, go back to **B**.)

Introducing *Peacemaker*ᔆᴹ and the Peace Table

Goals:
1. To introduce a peace mentor/heroine to help counteract violent heroes and heroines
2. To establish a friendship between *Peacemaker*ᔆᴹ and children
3. To provide reasons for being a peacemaker
4. To confirm it's O.K. to have a conflict
5. To develop a partnership between conflicting parties
6. To introduce the peace table

Materials:
1. Peacemaker Puppet™
2. Dialog after *I'm Mad* and *Peace Table* song from *We Can Solve it Peacefully* audiotape
3. Picture of the peace table at the United Nations (optional)
4. Peace table (A child-sized table with peace symbols sitting on it. Some ideas include a small plant, heart, bridge, small glass or ceramic animal, flower, or talking stick.)
5. Peace journals
6. Drum

Presentation:

1. Invite one of the children to gather the community with the sound of a softly beating drum.

2. Greet the children and say, "Today we are going to invite Peacemakerᔆᴹ to give the peacemaking lesson. Let's play the audiotape and see how the children on the tape invited *Peacemaker*ᔆᴹ to visit and help them. We can call Peacemakerᔆᴹ the same way! (Play the following dialog. It comes after the *I'm Mad* song:)

Nick: I hate it when people get mad. I even hate it when I get mad!
Shanti: Me too.
Nick: I guess I get scared. I always think something bad will happen.
Shanti: Yeah. . . and sometimes it does!
Nick: And we sang, "being mad isn't bad." Well, when I see people get mad, it seems pretty bad to me.
Rachel: I know what ya mean. . . . But I found out that when people get mad, it's sometimes because they have a problem they need to work out with someone. They just don't know how.
Nick: That's true.
Shanti: Yeah, I guess you're right.
Rachel: We just started using a peace table at home and at my school. That makes it a lot easier to work out our problems.
Nick: A peace table? What's that?
Shanti: Yeah, how do you solve your problems with a table? (laugh)
Rachel: Well, how about if I explain it to you?
Nick & Shanti: Cool / O.K.
Rachel: I'd like to ask my friend *Peacemaker*ᔆᴹ if she'll help me. She will if kids call her. Like this, *Peacemaker, Peacemaker*, will you come help us? Oh! There she is!
Peacemakerᔆᴹ**:** Hi kids! I heard you say you needed some help understanding the peace table. Well, we use the peace table when things aren't going right between two people and we want to work it out.

3. "How did the children on the tape call *Peacemaker*ᔆᴹ?" *Peacemaker, Peacemaker!* "Let's say it again." *Peacemaker, Peacemaker.*

4. Bring the Puppet out from behind your back. "Hi girls and boys! I am so excited about being invited here. Your teacher tells me you are a peacemaking class. Congratulations! I would like to get to know each one of you peacemakers. I'll come around the circle and shake your hand. When I shake your hand and look into your eyes, please tell me your name."

5. Greet each child with the Puppet. "I'm so happy to be able to meet you! Thank you for telling me your names! Being a peacemaker is the most important work in the whole world. I would like to use the talking stick to share our ideas about why being a peacemaker is such important work. Ms./Mr._____ (teacher's name) will write them down for us on chart paper." (You may need to switch the Puppet to your non-dominant hand, then write, *Reasons To Be A Peacemaker* on the top of the paper.) Pass the talking stick.

6. Record children's comments. Add any of the following reasons, or others you feel are important, if they haven't mentioned them yet.
a. So we know how to handle our conflicts nonviolently;
b. So we know how to take care of the earth, plants and animals;
c. So we can show respect to each other no matter what

skin, no matter what our age, or our abilities;

d. So we know how to be kind to others.

7. (Refer to their list) *Peacemaker^{SM}* says, "Yes! Look at all the important reasons there are to be peacemakers! Let's review them together." (Refer to their list. If the children are readers, point to each word and review by reading together. If they are nonreaders, ask them to repeat phrases after you.)

8. "I understand that you drew some pictures in your peace journals about some conflicts that can interrupt peace in your lives. I would like to see them. Who would like to share their picture?"

9. Choose a few volunteers. "Thank you for sharing your pictures with us! Conflicts happen to everybody. We just need to find a way to work them out. Sometimes people hurt each other's bodies or each other's feelings when they have a conflict. Peacemakers find ways to solve conflicts without violence.

10. "Before I became a peacemaker, I used to think I was right and the other person was wrong when I had a conflict or a problem. Now I've learned that most conflicts come from people having *different ideas* from each other. Instead of just thinking about my own ideas, I like to find out the other person's ideas too. That's why, now, I think about the other person as my *conflict partner* instead of my *enemy*. Can you say conflict partner[1] with me?" *Conflict partner.*

11. "I understand you've been learning to say, 'Please stop!' and, 'May I please work with you?' You've also learned to say, 'No' in a caring, or compassionate, way.

Those are all powerful ways to use words to be peacemakers and often can stop a conflict. When those words don't stop a conflict and your conflict partner and you still have a problem, peacemakers go to a special place, called the *peace table*, and work it out. In fact, our President (Premier, Prime Minister) and the leaders of other countries go to a peace table when they are working out a problem. (Show a picture of the peace table at the United Nations if you have one.) I brought a child-size peace table with me today so you can see it.

12. Unveil the peace table. *Peacemaker^{SM}* explains the rationale for the particular peace symbols she/he has chosen to put on it, and asks the children if they have any ideas of artifacts they would like to put on it. The children may wish to have turns bringing a peace symbol for it.

13. "I have a special song for you about the peace table. When we play the song, I would like to invite you to join me for a *peace march*. We can march around the peace table together!" Play the *Peace Table* song and lead the children in a march around the room.

14. "If I leave my peace table here, will you take care of it until I come back again and show you how to use it?" *Yes.* "Bye peacemakers." *Bye!* **(Put the cloth or veil cover back on the peace table until the entire process has been learned.)**

15. Teacher or child can close the gathering with the PEACE chant.

Empowerment of the Children:
1. Inviting the children to community
2. Their voices make *Peacemaker^{SM}* appear

3. Introducing themselves to *Peacemaker^{SM}*
4. Sharing their ideas about the importance of being peacemakers
5. Sharing their conflict pictures from their Peace Journals
6. Viewing another person as a conflict partner instead of enemy
7. Bringing a peace symbol for the peace table

Points of Interest:
1. Inviting children to community
2. Meeting *Peacemaker^{SM}*
3. Seeing a picture of the peace table at the United Nations
4. Making *Reasons To Be A Peacemaker Chart*
5. Sharing conflict pictures with *Peacemaker^{SM}*
6. Marching to music
7. Seeing the peace table being unveiled
8. Knowing *Peacemaker Puppet^{TM}* will be coming back to visit

Language Development:
1. Reasons to be a peacemaker
2. Conflict partner
3. Peace table
4. Peace symbol
5. Peace march
6. Different ideas

Extensions and Variations:
1. **Children draw reasons to be a peacemaker in their peace journals** or make a bulletin board called *Reasons To Be A Peacemaker* with their drawings.
2. **Children make a class collage of pictures of people helping each other** in various ways as suggested by the *Reasons To Be A Peacemaker* brainstorming chart.

[1.] D. Weeks, *Eight Essential Steps to Conflict Resolution,* (New York: G.P Putnam, 1992).

3. **Children trace or write the words** *Conflict Partner* on their conflict drawing.
4. **Practice songs,** *I'm Mad* **and** *Peace Table***.**
5. **Children paint peace symbols** or make them out of clay.
6. **Make a hanging mobile** of peace symbols.
7. **Make "stained glass" butterflies** to put in the window.
8. **Some suggested peace symbols** to work with: dove butterfly, rainbow, cloud, sun, flowers, heart, dolphins, tree. Brainstorm with the children and ask them for their ideas for peace symbols. Decorate your room for peace.

Teaching Tip:
Parents love to find out what their children are doing at preschool or school. Send a letter home, explaining the introduction of the peace table.

Dear Parent(s):
Today the children met the Peacemaker Puppet™ , who brought us a peace table for our classroom. We will be learning how to work with each other at the peace table and solve our problems nonviolently. The peace table is somewhat like the one used at the United Nations in New York. Next, the children will learn the steps for nonviolent conflict resolution.

Sincerely,
Your name

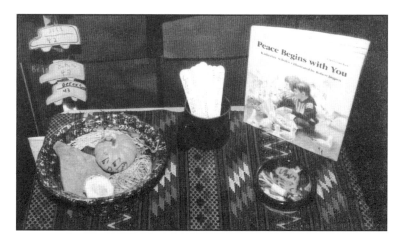

An example of a peace table in a second grade classroom.

Peacemaker's A,B,Cs of Conflict Resolution

A is **A**lways stop right now.

Ask to work it out somehow.

Become communicators, tell your part

Share the feelings in your heart.

B is **B**rainstorm things to do.

C is **C**hoose a plan to do.

D is **D**o it, then it's **E**,

Evaluate with you and me.

Additional Reading
S. Hopkins and J. Winters (eds., 1990). *Discover the World, Empowering Children to Value Themselves, Others and the Earth,* New Society, 4527 Springfield Ave., Phila., PA 19143.
B. Reardon (1987). *Education for a Global Responsibility: Teacher-Designed Curricula for Peace Education,* Teachers College Press, Teachers College, Columbia University, New York.
F. Schmidt and A. Friedman, *Peace Making Skills for Little Kids,* Peace Ed. Found., Miami FL.
W. Kreidler (1984). *Creative Conflict Resolution: Over 200 Activities for Keeping Peace in the Classroom,* Scott Foresman (Grades K-6).

Peace Table Step A, Part 1:
Always Stop Right Now! "Cool Off" Lesson

Goals:

1. To reinforce the "Please Stop!" lesson, with the concept of stopping oneself
2. To develop a cooling off strategy which can be used with or without teacher intervention
3. To help children find their own creative ways to return to peace when it is interrupted

Materials:

1. *Peace Table* song and *Always Cool Off* song from, *We Can Solve it Peacefully* audiotape
2. Two chairs labeled, "Peacethinking Chair" (these chairs will need to be available at all times)
3. Items to decorate the peacethinking chairs such as ribbon, crepe paper, feathers and pine cones which can be tied on, drawings of peace symbols which can be taped on, and/or anything else you and the children desire
4. Peacemaker Puppet™
5. Large piece of blank chart paper, or *Peacemaker's A,B,Cs, of Conflict Resolution™ (poster)*
6. Drum

Presentation:

1. Invite one of the children to gather the community with the sound of a softly beating drum.

2. Greet the children. Announce the visit of *Peacemaker^SM* enthusiastically.

3. Peacemaker^SM greets the children and says, "Today is the day we begin to learn how to use the peace table! Let's play the

Peace Table song again so we can learn some more of the words."

4. Play the song. Peacemaker Puppet™ asks, "Did you hear the letters A,B,C,D and E?" *Yes.* "Those are the letters we are going to use to learn about the peace table. What is the first letter of the alphabet?" *A* "That's right! It's also the first step for the peace table." (Teacher can put an A on a large sheet of blank paper, or point to step A on *Peacemaker's A,B,Cs of Conflict Resolution™*.)

5. "A is for 'Always stop right now!'" (Write *Always stop right now* under A on the paper and keep it posted throughout the time you are teaching the peace table process. If you have a ready-made poster, you may prefer to simply point to the first step.) "Let's say it together." *Always stop right now.*

Always Cool Off

A is cool off when you're too mad to talk.
I might like to sit, or just take a walk.
I breathe in and out, again and again,
Now I state the problem, so I understand.

Chorus:
Always, cool off, ask will you work this out?
Right left right, right left right, peacemakers
  are on the march.

Knowing the problem can be a bit tricky;
I can ask for help, if it seems really sticky.
A problem's not bad, just a challenge that's
  true
To work out with old friends, and work out
  with new.

Now I've cooled off and I know the task;
We've got a problem, so I must ask:
"Will you work this out, I want to be
  friends?"
Now we've got step A, let's sing it again.

"One more time."
Always stop right now.

6. "Sometimes we can feel so angry when we have a conflict we might want to push, hit, kick or even bite someone. When we remember to stop ourselves, or when someone asks us to, 'Please stop!' we give ourselves time to *cool off,* and we stop ourselves from hurting anyone.

7. "Stopping means *STOP right now!* when we're *soooo* angry. We can take a deep breath and take time to cool off so we can be ready to play or work again in a peaceful way. Stopping gives us time to think of how to solve the problem nonviolently. Let's listen to a song for step A. We can sing the chorus together." (Invite children to stand up and follow the Peacemaker Puppet™ around the room marching to the *Always Cool Off* song.)

8. "When peace gets interrupted, some children are sent to their room or asked to sit on time-out chairs. I wouldn't want to be sent to my room. I want to have a chance to cool off and think my problem through. I know people are very smart and have lots of ideas for getting back to peace, so I brought these *Peacethinking Chairs.*" (Show the labeled chairs.) "I like these chairs because they provide a

special place for us to cool off and think about how to get *back to peace.* They also can be used to think about and celebrate peace, even if we don't need to cool off. The more we think about peace, the more peaceful we become.

9. "Sometimes I have seen people sit on the Chair for just one minute and quickly get an idea of how to get back to peace. One boy I know, decided to apologize to his conflict partner for taking his work. He said he was sorry, and he would wait until his friend was finished playing with it before he would take a turn. He asked his friend to come get him when he was finished. Sometimes people like to sit on the Chair for a long time because it can take a while to calm down and think of some ideas.

10. "I'm going to try out the Peacethinking Chair (teacher and puppet sit on the chair, and model peaceful breathing). Who else would like to sit on one of the Peacethinking Chairs?" (Choose as many as you feel time allows.)

11. After they have sat in the Chair, continue: "There are some very beautiful items in this box to use to decorate the Peacethinking Chairs. Would you like to decorate them today?" *Yes!* "When I come back next time, I would like to see how you decorated them!

12. "Before leaving I would like to share my 'Peace Rap' with you." (Position chairs in the middle of the circle and ask the children to hold hands.) "Let's walk around the circle this way." (Determine your direction and start to move in a circular fashion) "The *Peace Rap* dance goes like this:

> ### *Peace Rap*
> by Rebecca A. Janke
>
> *I'm going over to the
> Peacethinking Chair.
> Gonna activate what's under my hair.
> I'm gonna think about ways to care.
> I'm gonna think about ways to share.
> Peace rap. Peace rap.*

"I must go now. Bye peacemakers." *Bye Peacemaker*SM.

13. Teacher: Show the children the choices of materials for decorating the chairs. Ask the children to work two at time in a peaceful and cooperative way. For a closing ceremony at the end of the session, you can do the *Peace Rap* dance again, around the decorated chairs.

Empowerment of the Children:
1. Inviting the children to community with the drum
2. Having the power to stop *oneself* from hurting anyone
3. Having a Peacethinking Chair to think about peace or return to peace
4. Determining the decorating of the Peacethinking Chair
5. Being able to calm oneself down
6. Having a specific place to cool off by oneself
7. Beginning the process of understanding personal responsibility

Points of Interest:
1. Drumming to invite the rest of the children to community
2. Seeing *Peacemaker Puppet*TM again
3. Having Peacethinking Chairs instead of time-out chairs
4. Dancing to the Peace Rap

5. Decorating the Peacethinking Chairs
6. Hearing the "Always Cool Off" strategy put to music
7. Sitting on the Peacethinking Chairs

Language Development:
1. Peacethinking Chair
2. Peace Rap
3. Always stop right now
4. Always cool off
5. Return to peace

Extensions and Variations:
1. **Brainstorm with the children other ways to cool off.** Post the list in the classroom.
2. **Do a puppet play with puppets who need to cool off.** The puppets cool off and then think of ways to return to peace. Use a conflict you have seen the children struggling with recently.
3. **Play the *We Can Solve It Peacefully* audiotape** while the children are working on an art activity.
4. **Practice the songs:** *I'm Mad, The Peace Table,* and *Always Cool Off*
5. **Teach the children this song, to the tune of** *If You're Happy and You Know it*
   If you're angry and you know it, stop and breathe. (repeat)
   If you're angry and you know it, You don't really need to blow it.
   If you're angry and you know it, stop and breathe.
6. **Children draw a peacethinking chair** in their peace journals.
7. **Practice the *Peace Rap*** a few minutes each day until the children have it memorized. It is fun to practice it with fingers snapping, clapping, rubbing hands together or in some way making a rhythmic sound.

8. **Send a letter home** to the parents explaining the Peacethinking Chair concept. Encourage the family to discuss other methods of cooling off, and suggest each family member develop her/his cooling off plan and post it on the refrigerator.

Additional reading:

Anger Control Problem-Solving Kit Center for Applied Psychology, PO Box 61586, King of Prussia, PA 19406 (Grades PreK-4).

Helping Children Learn Self-Control (brochure) NAEYC, 1509 16th St. NW, Washington DC 20036.

L. Slap-Shelton (1994). *Take a Deep Breath: The Kids Play Away Stress Book.* Center for Applied Psychology (Grades PreK-5).The Center for Applied Psychology has a catalog that includes many anger management games. PO Box 61586, King of Prussia, PA 19406.

Kids and Guns, *Kids and Guns = A Deadly Equation*, Kids and Guns, 1450 Northeast 2nd Ave. Room 523A, Miami, FL 33132 or 305-995-1986 (Grades K-6).

To Read With Children

L. Shapiro, *The Very Angry Day That Amy Didn't Have,* Center for Applied Psychology, PO Box 61586, King of Prussia, PA 19406 (grades PreK-3).

M. Mayer, *I Was So Mad* (1983). Western Publishing, Madison, WI 53404 (Grades PreK-1).

Cooperative Games

P. Huff, *The Cooperative Indoor and Outdoor Game Book* (1995). Scholastic, (Grades K-2).

T. Orlick, *The Cooperative Sports and Games Book* (1978). New York: Pantheon.

S. Bhava and J. Luvmour, *Everyone Wins,* New Society Publishers(Grades PreK-6).

A. Kohn, *No Contest: The Case Against Competition* (1986). New York: Houghton Mifflin.

Peace Table Step A, Part 2, *Ask to Work It Out* Lesson

Goals:

1. To empower children to take responsibility for initiating conflict resolution
2. To illustrate "Stopping right now"
3. To give children opportunities to practice and review peacemaking language skills as a means of preventing conflict
4. To encourage individual creativity for developing a peace plan while on the Peacethinking Chair
5. To demonstrate a technique for children who need additional support when their conflict partner refuses to participate in the problem solving process

Materials:

1. Two puppets with four blocks (Sarah and Jamie)
2. Peace table
3. Drum
4. *Always Cool Off* song from *We Can Solve it Peacefully* audiotape
5. Peacemaker Puppet™
6. The piece of large chart paper with *Always stop right now* written on it, or *Peacemaker's A,B,Cs, of Conflict Resolution™ (poster).*

Presentation:

1. Invite one of the children to gather the community with the sound of a softly beating drum.

2. Ask children to call *Peacemaker*^{SM} by saying, "Peacemaker, Peacemaker." *Peacemaker, Peacemaker.*

3. *Peacemaker Puppet™* greets the children. "Hello peacemakers! I like how you decorated your Peacethinking Chairs. You have two beautiful chairs for cooling off. Did you think of any ways to cool off besides using the Peacethinking Chairs?" (See **Extensions and Variations** numbers 1 and 7 in previous lesson.)

4. Listen to any ideas they may have had, and model active listening, (repeating their thoughts back to them).

5. "You are ready for the second part of Step A, *Ask to work it out.* Let's play the song, *Always Cool Off* again and listen for 'Ask to work it out.' If we have a problem, we want to work it out."

6. Play the tape and show excitement when you hear, "Ask to work it out." "Let's write that under *Always stop right now".* (Write it on the paper, or point to the words on the ready-made chart. Keep posted.)

7. "Sometimes we can't think of a way to solve the problem with our conflict partner when we are sitting on the Peacethinking Chair, or sometimes the idea we tried with our conflict partner doesn't work. When that happens it's time to *ask to work it out at the peace table."* (Have the peace table in the center of the community

or ask for two volunteers to bring the peace table to the community and carefully unveil it.)

8. "Remember the conflict the Sarah and Jamie puppets were having with the blocks?" *They had different ideas about how to use the blocks.* "That's right. Let's do some more puppet plays with them.

9. "Which two children would like to do a puppet play today with me?" Choose two volunteers. Coach them through the following scenes.

10. "Sarah and Jamie are playing peacefully with four blocks. Sarah begins to take the blocks away from Jamie and says, 'I'm going to build a tower. I need to take the blocks.' Jamie says, *'Please stop!'* Because it's a peacemaking classroom, Sarah stops."

11. *Peacemaker^SM* now asks the children to do the scene again: "This time when Sarah begins to take the blocks away, she uses compassionate assertiveness. She says, 'Jamie, I really want to work with all the blocks for awhile. Will you let me have all of them? *You can sit next to me.* O.K.?' Jamie says, 'Sure.'

12. "In the next scene, even though Sarah uses her compassionate assertiveness, Jamie doesn't want to share, and won't let Sarah have any blocks. Sarah says, 'Jamie, I really want to have all the blocks for awhile. Will you let me have them? Then you can sit next to me and watch.' Jamie says, 'No. I'm playing with them now. You can't have any.' Sarah pushes Jamie and says, 'I need the blocks.' Jamie is angry and says, 'I'm telling!' and pushes Sarah. Sarah starts to cry. They both need to stop and cool off.

Let's ask them where they would like to cool off.

13. "Jamie and Sarah decide to sit on the Peacethinking Chairs to *cool off*. While Jamie is there, he thinks of a *plan*. He will ask Sarah if he can work with her. After he's cooled off, Jamie asks Sarah, 'Can I work with you?' Sarah says, 'no.' They still have a conflict.

14. "Because Jamie's plan didn't work out, it's time for him to ask Sarah to go to the peace table, or he could go find some other work to do. Finding some other work to do is another way to be a peacemaker. However, today Jamie is more interested in working or playing with the blocks and wants to work this out with Sarah, so he is going to *ask to work it out.* He says, `Sarah, I'm having a conflict with you and I really want to work this out. Will you come to the peace table with me?' Sarah says, 'O.K.'"

15. *Peacemaker^SM* continues, "Sarah is going to come to the peace table when Jamie asks her because she knows when you're a peacemaker and someone invites you to the peace table, it means there is a *very* important problem and it needs to be worked out."

16. "It was interesting to see how Jamie did, *Ask to work it out.* The puppets are learning how to be peacemakers! When I come back next time we'll be ready to do Step B! Bye peacemakers." *Bye.*

17. Close with *Peacemaker Pledge* (see following page. Practice the *Pledge* often).

Empowerment Of The Children:
1. Inviting the children to community
2. Inviting *Peacemaker Puppet^TM* to join them
3. Sharing their ways of cooling off
4. Bringing the peace table to the community
5. Taking responsibility to go to the Peacethinking Chair
6. Asking one's conflict partner to participate in a plan for returning to peace
7. Asking one's conflict partner to come to the peace table
8. Asking the teacher for help *after* trying to return to peace

Points Of Interest:
1. Inviting *Peacemaker Puppet^TM*
2. Showing decorated Peacethinking Chairs
3. Listening for "Ask to work it out" in *Always Cool Off* song
4. Being puppeteers
5. Puppet playing alternatives using peacemaking language skills

Extensions and Variations:
1. **Put the puppets in the drama area** for children who didn't have a chance to be puppeteers to do puppet plays or for children who want to be puppeteers again.
2. **Color Step A** chart paper with peace symbols or with nonrepresentational coloring.
3. **Practice songs**: *I'm Mad*, *Peace Table* and *Always Cool Off*.
4. **To illustrate compassionate** behavior, ask a volunteer mother to come in and demonstrate giving a real baby a loving, caring bath.
5. **Set up a baby washing exercise** within the drama area.
6. **Go on a field trip** to the veterinarian and learn how she/he helps sick or injured animals.

7. **Invite other community peacemakers** to demonstrate how they care for and help others in the community. Record these in the Good Heart Journal.

8. **Make a bulletin board** of children's drawings, showing ways they are compassionate to each other and to adults.

Language Development:
1. *Ask to work it out*
2. Scene
3. Puppeteer
4. Plan
5. Compassionate assertiveness
6. *Peacemaker Pledge*
7. Mediator (See Teaching Tips)
8. Arbitrator (See Teaching Tips)

Teaching Tips: If a child refuses to go to the peace table the teacher can remind the child this is a peacemaking classroom where we care about each other. Explain, "If someone feels a need to ask us to go to the peace table they must be suffering, or hurt, or upset in some way. When this happens we need to show that we care and try to work it out. If the child still says, "No," you might say, "If you're not ready to come to the peace table now, maybe you need some more time to cool off. I'll check back with you later. When you are ready, invite your conflict partner to the peace table."

If the child still refuses, you can explain the role of a *mediator.* "Sometimes when two people are not able to work out a conflict by themselves, they ask a mediator to help. A mediator is a person who listens to each conflict partner, and helps them work it out. Would you like me to help you?

If the child continues to say, "No," you can explain the role of arbitrator. "An *arbitrator* or boss is used when people refuse to work it out, or can't work it out. **The arbitrator decides** how the problem will be worked out. Are you ready to go to the peace table and work this out yourselves, or do you need me to be an arbitrator?"

Another alternative is to suggest to her/him and the conflict partner that you will share the nature of the conflict with their parents or guardians since perhaps they would feel more comfortable talking it over with them first. Then let both children know that tomorrow there will be time to continue to work it out at the peace table. The key message is, "We need to work this out."

Additional Reading
P. Prutzman, et. al. (1978). *The Friendly Classroom for a Small Planet,* New Society Publishers, 4527 Springfield Ave., Phila. PA 19143 (Grades PreK-3).

G. Sadalla, M. Holmberg, and J. Holligon. *Conflict Resolution: Elementary School Curriculum, Community Board Program,* 1540 Market Street, Suite 490, San Francisco, CA 94102.

U. Palomares and B. Logan, *A Curriculum on Conflict Management.* Human Development Training Institute, 7574 University Ave. LaMesa, CA 92041 (Grades K-6).

To Read With Children
R. Johnson and D. Johnson, *Della the Dinosaur Talks About Violence and Anger Management.* Johnson Institute, 7205 Ohms Lane, Mpls, MN 55439 (Grades PreK-6).

E. Fugitt, *He Hit Me Back First.* Jalmar Press (Grades (PreK-4).

J. W. Berry (1984). *Let's Talk About Fighting* Childrens Pr., Chicago IL.

J. Udry, *Let's Be Enemies,* Harper and Row, New York (PreK-1).

The Peacemaker Pledge
by Julie P. Peterson

I promise to be a peacemaker, in class, at home, and at play.
Treating others with care and respect, and in my special way,
Taking care of myself and the earth, and showing that I'm able
And brave enough when there's conflict, to march to the peace table.

Peace Table Step B, Part 1
Become Communicators Lesson

Introduction:

One of the most difficult skills for adults to learn and practice is saying effective I-messages. However, when children learn this skill, they often take to it readily. With the help of *Peacemaker's Conflict Resolution Cubes*[TM], the children will learn this skill with astounding speed. (See teaching tips below.) If you don't have the cubes, spend time helping the children learn to identify their feelings, then invite them to describe them to others.

Children from some cultures may find using I-messages challenging. Children who speak in terms of "we" instead of "I" (more common among some indigenous cultures), and those who have been taught never to talk about their feelings, may have particular difficulty with it. It is important to be sensitive to the needs of each individual child. Take some time, before you introduce this lesson, to study and reflect upon the conflict resolution styles of each child's family and culture. You may want to read, *Understanding the Multicultural Experience in Early Childhood Education*, edited by Olivia N. Sayaclo and Bernard Spodel, NAEYC, 1983. You also may want to ask for information and/or advice from someone who is familiar with the cultural influences in the child's life. It is important to know how to be most respectful to each child, while still conveying the essence of the lesson.

Steps for using an I-message and active listening:

At the peace table, each child, one at a time, gives an "I-message" with three components.
1. I feel____
2. when ____
3. because___.
The listener (conflict partner) then shows the I-message has been heard by doing active listening (repeating or paraphrasing).

Goals:
1. To introduce beginning concepts of taking responsibility for one's feelings
2. To empower children to communicate their feelings in an appropriate manner
3. To introduce and practice the skills for I-messages and active listening

Materials:
1. *Peacemaker's Conflict Resolution Cubes*[TM]
2. *Peacemaker Puppet*[TM]
3. Drum
4. Another large piece of chart paper, or *Peacemaker's A,B,Cs of Conflict Resolution*[TM] (poster).
5. *We Can Solve it Peacefully*, audiotape, dialog after *Celebrate*

Presentation:

1. Invite one of the children to gather the community with the sound of a softly beating drum.

2. Ask the children to call *Peacemaker*[SM] by saying, *"Peacemaker, Peacemaker."*

3. *Peacemaker*[SM] appears, greets the children and says, "You did such a good job of learning Step A, you are ready for the next step! Before we learn it, let's say Step A together.
A is _____ (always stop right now)
and_____(ask to work it out somehow). That was fun to say together! What letter comes after A?" *B* "Yes." Put on a piece of chart paper or point to ready-made chart. "B is *Become Communicators.*"

4. "When I go to the peace table I become a communicator because my conflict partner needs to know how I feel and I need to know how she or he feels. We do this by giving each other `I-messages.' Jamie and Sarah are ready to become communicators now. An I-message for Jamie might go like this: *I feel angry when all the blocks are taken away from me.* Sarah might say, *I feel angry when I can't make a tower when I want to.*"

5. "Today, we will play a game with conflict resolution cubes so we know how to say I-Messages to each other This is better than saying, `You make me mad,'

because when we have a feeling it belongs to us, not the other person. That's why it's important to say *I* instead of *you*. Peacemakers *take responsibility* for their own feelings."

6. Show the cube with the uncomfortable feeling faces. *Peacemaker*^{SM} names all the feelings on the cube and shows them to the children. "Who would like to roll this cube and see which feeling face we get?" Choose a volunteer. Now we say, `I feel _____'" (name the feeling on the cube -- either angry, sad, frustrated, worried, lonely, or hurt).

7. Show the cube with the uncomfortable *scenarios*. "This cube has a story on each side. Each person describes what he or she sees as the story. Who would like to roll the story cube?" The child who rolled it, determines the nature of the conflict and describes it to the community. For example, he or she might say "somebody is kicking blocks over." Continue until several children have rolled the cube and described a scenario.

8. "O.K.! Let's put the first cube with the story cube and say an I-Message. *I feel angry when someone kicks my blocks over.*" Continue to play the I-message game for a few more rounds or until everyone in the group has had a turn to roll the cubes and say an I-message.

9. "Now you know how to become communicators, say your part, share the feelings in your heart." Point to those words on the chart.

10. To make sure we have heard and understood our conflict partner's I-message, it's a good idea to repeat what our partner said.

Let's practice. I'll say an I-message, and your teacher will do *active listening* and repeat it back to me."

11. *Peacemaker Puppet*^{TM} says, "I feel sad when someone won't play with me, because then I think I'm left all alone." Teacher says, "Oh, you feel sad when someone won't play with you because you think you are left all alone?" *Peacemaker* answers, "Yes."

12. Practice some more I-messages with the cubes to end the session.

Session 2 or continue:
1. Let's listen to the children on the tape use I-messages and active listening." Put on the *We Can Solve it Peacefully* tape dialog after *Celebrate*. Show nonverbal excitement when you hear the I-messages and active listening. You may want to play it more than once, stopping the tape to repeat the I-messages and the active listening parts.

2. "Let's try it with a puppet play. Who, would like to get Sarah and Jamie so we can help them with their I-messages?" Choose two volunteers. "When they practice their I-messages, they are going to do active listening, too. When Jamie says his I-message, Sarah is going to tell him what she heard. Then, when Sarah says her I-message, Jamie is going to say what he heard."

3. Coach the children through this scene. Jamie says, "I feel angry when I can't have any of the blocks. Sarah says, "You feel angry when you can't have any blocks?" Jamie says, "Yes." Sarah says, "I feel angry when I can't build what I want to build. Jamie says, "You

feel angry when you can't build what you want to build?" Sarah says, "Yes."
4. *Peacemaker Puppet*^{TM} *says:* "Sarah and Jamie have *become communicators*! Let's clap for our puppeteers.

5. "Now let's try saying our own I-message with just the face cube." Ask a volunteer to roll a cube. "You rolled sad. What is something that you feel sad about when it happens?" Child might say, "I feel sad, when I'm not invited to play with the older kids." Continue until all children have had a turn at giving personal I-messages, or choose a few volunteers.

6. "Next time when I come back we'll do the second part of Step B, Brainstorm! Bye peacemakers." *Bye.*

7. Close with Peace chant. P - E - A - C - E (repeat 2x). Peace, Peace, Peace.

Empowerment of the Children:
1. Beginning to learn words to describe their feelings
3. Taking responsibility for one's own feelings when saying an I-message
4. Interpreting the conflict stories on the scenarios cube
5. Doing a puppet play
6. Having feelings validated through active listening

Points of Interest:
1. Listening to the children on the tape
2. Playing a cube game
3. Doing a puppet play
4. Saying their own I-message
5. Interpreting stories of conflict
6. Watching a puppet play performed by peers
7. Finding out what Jamie and Sarah will say

Language Development:

1. Become communicators
2. I-message (I feel ____ when ____ because ____.)
3. Active listening
4. Responsibility
5. Conflict Resolution Cubes™

Extensions and Variations:

1. **Practice active listening in cooperative pairs** about any topic.
2. **Play telephone** at community time. One child whispers a message into the ear of child next to him/her. The receiving child whispers the message to the child on her/his right and so on until the message has gone around the entire circle. The last child receiving it states what she/he heard and first child verifies if it was the original message.
3. **Invite children to draw a conflict story** in their peace journal and make up an I-Message for each person.
4. **Practice the songs**: *I'm Mad, Peace Table*, and *Always Cool Off*. Listen to the dialogs.
5. **Share with children the Conflict Resolution Skip** (below -- to tune of *Skip to My Lou*)

Someone takes my blocks
what'll I do? (3 times)
Say 'please stop' my darling.

Someone won't stop what'll I
do? (3 times)
Get an adult my darling.

Someone is angry, what'll she
do? (3 times)
Go cool off my darling.

(The children can make up additional verses.)

Teaching Tips:

Three-year-olds will do a simpler version of I-messages than older children. Most often, three-year-olds will be successful with the first component of the I-message, such as in this statement: **"I feel** mad."

Four-year-olds are able to say the first two components: **I feel** mad **when** somebody takes my blocks.

Five-year-olds attempt to be successful with all three components: **I feel** mad **when** somebody takes my blocks, **because** I wanted to make something cool with them. Or: "**I feel** angry **when** the toy I wanted to play with is always being used by someone else, **because** I haven't had a turn yet." Or: "**I feel** frustrated **when** I can't play with toys that look fun **because** I like those toys too."

Five-year-olds can do active listening very capably. With younger children, you can help them with their active listening by asking some questions, such as, "Did Jim say he felt sad, or did he say he felt lonely, when he can't play with you?"

Put the cubes in the drama area. This will afford the children further practice to continue playing this game and/or implementing I-messages into their self-initiated role plays.

Additional Reading

M. Bauer, *Peace Education at Spruce Street School*, Spruce Street School, 701 Spruce St., Saux City, WI 53583

National School Safety Center, *Set Straight on Bullies*, 4165 Thousand Oaks Blvd., Suite 290, Westlake Village, CA 91362

To Read With Children:

J. Havill, *Jamaica and Brianna*, Scholastic Inc., P.O. Box 7502 Jefferson City, MO 65102

J. Vigra Whitman (1979). *The Hiding House*, Whitman.

C. Zolotow (1969). *The Hating Book*, Harper and Row.

J. Cowky (1969). *The Duck in the Gun,* Doubleday.

J. Silver (1978). *Rebecca, Margaret and Nasty Annie*, Platt and Murk.

R. Hoban (1964). *The Sorely Trying Day,* Harper and Row.

H. Hamada (1967). *Tears of the Dragon*, Parents, Can be borrowed from the Philadelphia Yearly Meeting Library, 1515 Cherry Street, Philadelphia, PA 19102.

M. Leach (1961). *Noodles, Nitwits and Numskulls*, William Collins.

K. Iwamura (1980/1984). *Ton and Pon.* New York: Bradbury.

T. Webster-Doyle, *Why is Everybody Always Picking on Me? A Guide to Handling Bullies,* Atrium Publications, PO Box 938, Ojai, CA 93023. (Grades 2-6).

T. Webster-Doyle, *Maze of the Fire Dragon*, Atrium Publications

B. Turkk (1965). *Obadiah the Bold,* Viking (PreK-3).

W. O. Steele (1978). *The War Party*, Harcourt, Brace, Javanovich.

J. Erskine (1978). *The Snowman*, Crown (Grades PreK- 1).

T. Geisel, (1971) *The Lorax*, Random House (Grades PreK-6).

O. Wilde (1979). *The Selfish Giant*, McGraw Hill.

C. Zolotow (1963). *The Quarreling Book*, Harper and Row (Grades PreK-2).

F. McNulty (1980). *The Elephant Who Couldn't Forget*, Harper and Row (Grades PreK-3).

M.W. Shermat (1975). *Walter the Wolf*, Scholastic Book Service, PO Box 7502, Jefferson City, MO 65102 (Grades PreK-3).

Developing Vocabulary and Understanding of Feelings

It is important to help children develop their vocabulary so they can more accurately describe their *feeling state* and understand other's choice of words when they describe their feeling state. A large empty photo book is an excellent resource for making a "feelings book." The children can cut pictures from magazines and sort them into the four categories which represent the basic feelings: glad, mad, sad and scared. Use these four words as chapter headings in the feelings book.

With younger children, sorting the pictures into these four headings is the first step. When they are about four- or five-years-old, they may be ready to explore some additional descriptive words. Ask the children if they have another word that might describe the picture for glad, mad, sad or scared. This way children develop a vocabulary of common feelings, and will understand how these feelings fit into their basic, familiar framework of glad, sad, mad and scared. Introduce any words from the list (below) that the children don't offer on their own. Then you can compile "chapters" in the *Feelings Book*.

For example, when compiling the *Mad* chapter, you can find and label different pictures as frustrated, upset, aggravated, exasperated, angry, infuriated, and so on. Labels on the pictures in the *Glad* chapter will include happy, content, excited, and so on.

By keeping the *Feelings Book* in the peace library, the children can look at it whenever they want. It also serves as a pictorial resource for the teacher when providing "feelings" activities. Children can be encouraged to use the *Feelings Book* for portraying different feelings for conflict resolution role plays.

GLAD: Feelings likely to be present when needs are satisfied Some additional words to describe GLAD.

MAD, SAD, SCARED: Feelings likely to be present when needs are not satisfied:

			Mad	Sad	Scared
happy	grateful	moved	frustrated	concerned	grief
content	interested	amazed	upset	guilty	worried
confident	delighted	excited	aggravated	disturbed	hurt
elated	encouraged	eager	exasperated	embarrassed	anxious
comfortable	stimulated	touched	irritated	anguished	afraid
involved	intrigued	inspired	angry	unhappy	nervous
satisfied	secure	joyful	crazed	lonely	uneasy
appreciative	fulfilled	peaceful	infuriated	distressed	upset

Sometimes we adults, as well as children, use words that are actually judgments of our feelings, or someone's motives. "I feel hopeless, incompetent, worthless, bad," is really describing our *analysis* of our feeling of sadness. These are intellectual responses to our feelings, often not describing our own feelings, but describing the blame we would like to place on others. This outer-directed expression of feelings leads to defensive communications. For example: "I feel *sad* when someone I like won't play with me," sounds a lot different than, "I feel *worthless* when someone I like won't play with me." The latter sounds accusatory; as if someone can inflict a sense of worthlessness. It does not exemplify responsibility for one's own feelings.

Here's another example: I feel mistreated, undervalued, inadequate or ignored. These words imply an unspoken, "by you." They don't help people identify their own root feelings. In order to promote personal responsibility and growth, it is helpful to role model and encourage children to use true feelings words. You might like to post the above list of words for your reference.

[1.] Marshal Rosenberg and the staff at the Bay Area Center for Nonviolent Communications, San Francisco, CA are very helpful at teaching effective nonviolent ways to express feelings. Their workshops are highly recommended for adults.

Peace Table Step B, Part 2: Brainstorm Lesson

We're Having a Brainstorm

We each tell our feelings, what do we get?
I'm sad, lonely, hurt, mad, or something like that.
It really takes practice to speak from the heart.
I know you can do it you're so very smart.

When I hear your feelings I listen with my ears
I listen with my heart, I listen through my fears
Then I say it back, I say, this is what I heard. . .
I never need to fight, I can always use a word.

After each feeling we have has been said,
We start getting lots of ideas in our heads.
This is brainstorming, it's fun to do,
We use our brains and we use our hearts too.

We're having a brainstorm, not a rainstorm,
it's brainstorming today.

Introduction:

Brainstorming is a key component to the problem solving process. It involves **uncensored** generation of ideas -- wise and silly -- allowing the children to expand their creativity. Brainstorming is critical in developing children's sense that we have choices when faced with conflict. The children learn there are possible solutions that meet some or all of each conflict partner's needs, and there are alternatives to violence.

Brainstorming can be a private activity when used by two individuals (with a coach in the beginning) at the peace table, or the children can be helped by the community through a "fishbowl" technique. This is a time for those in conflict to attempt to solve the problem with the group, if group involvement is agreed upon. The group becomes involved in the brainstorming, generating ideas for solutions to the problem. Because many of the children's

favorite TV and movie characters choose violent solutions to their problems, these programs provide an opportunity to practice brainstorming. We might begin by asking the children if a certain character is a peacemaker. When we hear, "No," we tell them they have the power to change the story by becoming "peace authors," "peace storytellers," or "peace illustrators." At first, when invited to choose an alternative to violence for the action figures from TV shows, many children will say, "No, no, no, that's not the way it goes! They don't do that!"

Children often are not acting out their own solutions to conflict but are repeating a television, video, or story script. They are being scripted or "brainwashed" into believing violence is the *usual* solution to a problem, and characters are all "bad" or all "good." In order to help them gain some perspective, and

realize that nonviolence, or peace, is the standard, you might brainstorm using some questions like the following two examples:

1. "What could the Power Rangers do differently to show they are peacemakers?" As the children realize that the Power Rangers haven't explored all their alternatives to violence, they begin to develop media literacy.
2. "What do you think one of the bad guys would do if his little girl or little boy got hurt?" If they put the "bad guy" in the role of nurturer, it gives them permission to see themselves as peacemakers, even through they may identify with the "bad guy."

Providing activities to draw, rewrite, or retell the stories of violence they have seen on television, calls children to practice developing their own creative alternatives to violence.

For non-writers the teacher records the peacemaking story. (See Additional Reading at the end of this session, for resources about publishing the children's stories.)

Goals:
1. To have children gain skills for brainstorming
2. To encourage creativity during conflict
3. To show that there is a peaceful choice
4. To share the techniques of fishbowl brainstorming

Materials:
1. *We're Having A Brainstorm*, song from *We Can Solve it Peacefully* audiotape
2. Pencil
3. Two puppets (Sarah and Jamie)
4. Peace table
5. *Peacemaker* Puppet
6. Drum
7. Talking stick
8. Chart paper from previous lessons or *Peacemaker's A,B,Cs of Conflict Resolution*™ (poster)

Presentation:

1. Invite one of the children to gather the community with the sound of a softly beating drum.

2. Children invite *Peacemaker*ˢᴹ.

3. *Peacemaker*ˢᴹ greets the children and says, "Last time I was here, Sarah and Jamie learned how to become communicators and gave each other an I-Message. Who would like to describe Sarah and Jamie's conflict so we can all remember?" Choose a volunteer.

"Yes. They had different ideas about how they wanted to use the blocks.

4. "What was Jamie's I-Message?" Choose a volunteer. (Jamie said, "I feel angry when I can't have any of the blocks.") "What was Sarah's I-Message?" Choose a volunteer. (Sarah said, "I feel angry when I can't build what I want to build.")

5. "Because they have different ideas about using the blocks, the second part of Step B, *Brainstorm*, will be helpful for them to come up with some ideas of how to solve this problem." (Write *Brainstorm* on the paper under *Become Communicators* or refer to ready-made chart.)

6. "Let's listen to a song about sharing or telling our feelings, listening actively, and brainstorming." (Play *We're Having A Brainstorm*.)

7. "Did you hear how *Peacemaker*ˢᴹ sang about feelings? She sang about I-messages and about active listening. I'll say the words: (refer to song on previous page).

8. "Brainstorming is one of my favorite things to do because we get to use our *imaginations*! It doesn't matter if our ideas are silly. We just keep thinking of more and more ideas until we run out of them. We peacemakers use our brains to try to think of peaceful or nonviolent ways to solve our problems.

9. "Before we work with Sarah and Jamie, let's play a game to practice brainstorming. I'll pass around a pencil and we'll think of ideas about what this pencil could be used for, instead of just writing."

10. Record the ideas on a big sheet of paper, labeled, *Pencil Brainstorming*. Keep it posted in the classroom for a week or two. "Let's see how many ideas we can get." Pass the pencil like you would a talking stick. Ask children to look at it and feel it and use their wildest imaginations. Remind them they can pass if they can't think of anything right now.

11. "Oh! We have five ideas. Let's try to get three more!" (It's a boat, a hair curler, it holds up a planet, it's a spinner, a digger, a fishing pole, a bat for a ping pong ball, a hammer, a butter knife, or a flag pole are some ideas that have been offered by children) "Congratulations!"

12. "We've been learning to brainstorm so we can think of lots of ways to solve a problem with our conflict partner at the peace table. Now, let's try brainstorming with Sarah and Jamie so they can solve their conflict."

13. Put the peace table in the center of the community and unveil it. Invite the children to bring Sarah and Jamie to the peace table.

14. "Sarah and Jamie could do their own brainstorming at the peace table, but they have invited us to do *fishbowl brainstorming*. When the whole community helps with brainstorming it is called 'fishbowl brainstorming.' The two people who are having the conflict show us their conflict, like it's in a glass fishbowl, and we become the people looking at the fishbowl.

15. "Let's use the talking stick so everyone can have a chance to think and share ideas." Pass the talking stick.

16. Write down the children's ideas on a piece of chart paper titled, *Fishbowl Brainstorming.* "Look at all the ideas we have!

17. "The next step in using the peace table is C - *Choose.* When I see you next time, we'll see which idea Sarah and Jamie want to choose. I can hardly wait! Bye Peacemakers.

18. Close with Peace chant.

Empowerment of the Children:
1. There are many ideas of ways to solve problems.
2. Generating alternatives to violence

Points of Interest:
1. *We're Having a Brainstorm* song, especially hearing the storm
2. Brainstorming game with pencil
3. Participating in fishbowl brainstorming
4. Anticipating Sarah's and Jamie's choice

Language Development:
1. Brainstorm
2. Imagination
3. Choose
4. Ideas
5. Fishbowl brainstorming
6. Alternatives
7. Peace author
8. Peace storyteller
9. Peace illustrator or artist

Extensions and Variations:
1. **Play brainstorming games with other objects.** Here is a simple exercise: "Here's a bracelet. I wear it on my wrist. Let's use our imaginations and think about what else we could do with this bracelet (If possible, pass the item around the circle, like a talking stick, and only the person who has the item can speak). . . I think it could be a spaceship. . . I think it could be a magic ring, how about a dog collar?. . ."
2. **Tell about a current event in the world news** and have children brainstorm peaceful solutions to it.
3. **Brainstorm nonviolent choices for a read-aloud story.**
4. **Color the "B" paper with peace symbols.**
5. **Practice the songs:** *I'm Mad, Peace Table, Always Cool Off,* and *Brainstorming.*
6. **Make an object out of clay** and have a friend brainstorm what it might be.
7. **When a child shows you something he/she made, ask, "Does it do anything else?"** to extend and expand the child's opportunity for creative thinking.

Teaching Tips:
It is important for the children to try to generate their own ideas at the peace table for maximum empowerment. However, if the children are unable to brainstorm any options after you encourage them to do so a few times, simply jump start them with one or two ideas and let them try again.

If the children are unable to brainstorm any options because they feel their needs are opposing, the teacher can help the brainstorming process by pointing out **hidden commonalities**. For example, maybe two children want to play with the same toy or do the same work. The teacher can mention a commonality by saying, "There are other children here who aren't interested in this toy, but <u>both</u> of you are, and you <u>agree</u> it is fun. Since both of you <u>agree</u> it is fun, what can people do when they <u>both</u> like something and they <u>both</u> want a chance to use it?"

To find hidden commonalities it is helpful to ask the children their reasons for wanting to do an activity. For example, two children begin to fight about who stirs the cookie dough first. One child might say, "I want to give these to my mom for a surprise when she picks me up today." The other child may say, "I want to bake so we can have these cookies for snack." The teacher hears the hidden commonality and says, "Since both of you want to work very hard to be able to share, which is a peaceful thing to do, what do you think we can do to stir the dough peacefully?"

Sometimes brainstorming on the spot precludes the necessity of going to the peace table. **Remember, the children brainstorm solutions to their own problems. We are facilitators.**

List all brainstorm ideas, even ones that may be inappropriate. In the next lesson we'll discuss some ways for sorting through the ideas.

Peace Table Step C: Choose Lesson

Introduction:

Choosing a solution often flows out of the brainstorming step quite naturally. The children may immediately realize they have brainstormed an agreeable solution, and have *chosen* without a formal decision- evaluation process.

Brainstormed solutions to some problems require considerable evaluation in terms of their consequences. To do this, take another big piece of chart paper, and place it next to your brainstorming list. Write "Consequences" on the top and make three columns labeled as follows: Good for me?/Good for the Group?/What might happen [if this idea were chosen?]. Encourage the children to evaluate the choices, using these questions, as you write their comments in the appropriate column.

More specific questions are sometimes necessary: Is it unkind? Is it hurtful? Is it unfair? Is it dishonest (or illegal)? In this way, unworkable suggestions can be removed from the list.

Goals:

1. To discover that each choice we make has a consequence
2. To look at all the brainstorm ideas before making a choice
3. To learn to choose a solution which considers the needs of all involved -- a win-win solution
4. To learn that making a choice is developing a plan with your conflict partner
5. To practice consensus/consent decision-making

Materials:

1. *When You Ch, Ch, Ch, Ch Choose* from *We Can Solve it Peacefully*
2. Peacemaker Puppet™
3. Peace Table
5. Two puppets (Sarah and Jamie)
6. Drum
7. Fishbowl Brainstorming chart from previous lesson
8. Chart paper from lessons A and B, and a new sheet for lesson C, or *Peacemaker's A,B,Cs of Conflict Resolution™* (poster)

Presentation:

1. Choose a child to invite children to community with a drum.

2. Children invite *Peacemaker^SM* to community. *Peacemaker^SM* greets the children and says, "Today is the day we find out what Sarah and Jamie are going to choose as the solution to their conflict!" So far we have learned Step A, *Always stop right now and Ask to work it out somehow* and Step B, *Become communicators, say your part, share the feelings in your heart*, and B is *Brainstorm things to do*. Now, what letter comes after B?" C "Yes! The next step starts with the letter C. It is Choose." (Refer to the A and B chart papers or the ready-made chart.) Let's add a C to our paper." Write "Choose a plan to do."

3. "C sounds like (s) and also like (k) but when you put it with H it sounds like (ch). Can you help me on the *Ch, Ch, Ch, Ch, Choose* song?" *Sure!* "Let's listen to the tape and sing along." (Play tape.)

4. Choose two volunteers to bring the Sarah and Jamie puppets to the peace table located in the center of the community. Unveil the peace table.

5. "In order for Sarah and Jamie to choose a solution to their problem, they need to think about what would happen, or what might be the consequences for each idea listed on the Fishbowl Brainstorming chart. Let's write `Consequences' under `Choose.' When peacemakers think about the consequences they are thinking through the ideas very carefully. I'll read the first idea and you tell me what might happen if Jamie and Sarah chose that one. Then I'll read the second idea and we'll think about the consequences. We'll keep doing this until we've talked about each idea.

6. "Sarah and Jamie are working to choose a win-win solution. A win-win solution is a plan they both like." At this point, remind the children that we make decisions by consensus or consent. "Both of the conflict partners must be willing to choose an idea, or think it is good enough that they can *consent* or *agree* to it, in order for us to be ready to choose that solution. Who would like to be our puppeteers today?" Choose two children.

7. Invite the two puppeteers to go over the consequence chart with you. Ask them "Is it good for me? /Good for the group?/What might happen?" about each choice. The two puppeteers choose by consensus. "Sarah and Jamie! You did Step C, Choose. Congratulations! Let's clap for these conflict partners. Remember, if they didn't like any of these ideas, they could go back to B and brainstorm until they found a win-win solution. This time they did find a win-win solution. Hooray!"

8. Close with Peace chant.

Empowerment of the Children:
1. Inviting children to community
2. Inviting *Peacemaker*[SM] to visit
3. Thinking about consequences for themselves

Points of Interest:
1. The ch, ch, ch, ch sound related to Step C, Choose
2. Singing the *When You Ch, Ch, Ch, Ch Choose* song
3. Being puppeteers
4. Thinking about consequences
5. Discovering what Sarah and Jamie choose

Language Development:
1. choose
2. consequence
3. win-win solution
4. consent or agree

Teaching Tip: If two children are unable to find a win-win solution, it may be necessary to put the object of dispute away so children can more clearly focus on finding a win-win solution.

Extensions and Variations:
1. **Role play a disagreement** about what to choose. The puppets eventually choose after much debate.
2. **Role play an actual situation** that has occurred in the classroom.
3. **Role play needing an arbitrator.** (See information about arbitrators in the **Teaching Tips** section of the Peace Table Step A, Part 2, Ask to Work it Out Lesson.)
4. **Color the "C" part of the chart** paper with peace symbols
5. **Practice the songs**, *I'm Mad, Peace Table, Always Cool Off,* and *When You Ch, Ch, Ch Ch Choose,* **and listen to the Dialog after** *Celebrate.*

When You Ch Ch Ch Ch Choose

Now when you ch ch ch ch choose,
You leave the b b b b blues,
'Cause when you ch ch ch ch choose,
You've solved the problem. (repeat)

Choosing a solution can be hard to do,
But after all you care for me, and I for you.
We kinda have a feeling about which one will do
'cause we listened very carefully, and thought it through.

Sometimes I have a problem and I don't know the way out,
We're finished with our brainstorm and I want to pout.
I don't like any choices, nothing works for me
That's when I remember to go back to B!

If we can't choose together, we might be too tired;
We can try it again later, yes, it is required.
We're peacemakers together, we will work it out,
'Cause peacemaking, peacemaking's what it's all about.

Additional Reading
L. King and D. Stowall, *Classroom Publishing,* Zephyr Press, 3316 N. Chapel Ave. PO Box 66006-B Tucson, AZ 85728-6006.

Easy Book, Macintosh Software, Prufrock Press, PO Box 8813 Waco, TX 76714-8813.

My Own Stories, Macintosh Software, Prufrock Press.

How to Capture Live Authors and Bring Them to Your School, Prufrock Press.

S. Fluck, *How to Organize a Peace Essay Contest in Your Community,* can be borrowed from the Philadelphia Yearly Meeting Library.

Lakeshore Learning Materials, *Making Big Books with Children.* Volumes I & II sold separately. Lakeshore Learning Materials, 2629 E. Dominguez St., Carson, CA 90749 or call 800-421-5354.

Peace Heroes Young Voices Essay Contest (Grades 2-6). Peace Education Foundation, Inc. PO Box 19-1153, Miami Beach, FL 33119 or call 1-800-749-8838.

M. Harmin, *Spunjz: Language Arts Activities for Self Awareness,* Zephyr Press.

Resources to Share With Children
C.W. More-Slater, *Dana Doesn't Like Guns Anymore,* Friendship Press (Grades PreK-4).

J. Conaway (1977). *I'll Get Even,* Raintree Publishers (Grades PreK-2).

E. Crary, *I Can't Wait / I Want It / I Want to Play / My Name is Not Dummy,* all published by Parenting Press (Grades PreK-2).

Rudeness, Whining and Bickering (video) Kimbo Educational, PO Box 477, Dept. V, Long Branch, NJ 07740.

A. Aborn, *Everything I Do You Blame on Me!* Center.for Applied Psychology (K-6).

L. Shapiro, *Sometimes I Like to Fight, But I Don't Do It Much Anymore,* Center for Applied Psychology (Grades PreK-5).

K. Scholes (1991). *Peace Begins With You,* Sierra Club Books, 7340 Polk St., San Francisco, CA 94109 415-923-5603.

We Can Solve it Peacefully, Dialog After *Celebrate*

Peacemaker: Does anybody have a problem we can try to solve peacefully?

Nick: I do.

Peacemaker: Oh, well, can you tell us about it?

Nick: Yes. I have a problem with Jackson. I was playing with the marble game with Mary and Jessica yesterday, and he came over and started taking pieces and playing with our stuff, and wrecked our work. I was really mad.

Peacemaker: Hmmm, are you still really mad? Do you need to cool off some more?

Nick: No, I was, but I've cooled off. But I still have a problem. Jackson always wrecks my work.

Peacemaker: Well, let's find out if Jackson wants to work this out?. Remember in step A we *Ask to work it out?*

Nick: Yes. Jackson, can we work this out someway?

Jackson: I suppose.

Peacemaker: Jackson, what do you think the problem is?

Jackson: I'm always being left out.

Peacemaker. So what I hear is, Jackson and Nick have different ideas about how they want to play together. Does that sound right?

Jackson/Nick: Yes

Peacemaker: O.K. Now, besides asking to work it out and saying the problem, what else do we do in step A?

Nick: Well, next we say how we feel.

Peacemaker: That's right. (singing) *Let's each tell our feelings* Good. Go ahead.

Nick: I feel angry **when** someone messes up my work **because** I was trying to make something really cool.

Jackson: O.K. You feel angry when your work's messed up.

Nick: Right.

Jackson: I feel lonely **when** kids don't let me play with them, **because** I think nobody likes me.

Nick: You feel lonely?

Jackson: Yes.

Nick: We didn't know that.

Peacemaker: O.K. Now that we know how you each feel, let's do B, brainstorm some ways to solve this problem.

Nick: O.K. Let's see, to brainstorm means to get ideas and I have an idea. Jackson could just ask to work with us.

Jackson: Or you could ask me to play with you.

Nick: Yes, but sometimes I might want to play alone. Then I'll say I don't want to play right now. O.K.?

Jackson: O.K. but my feelings might be hurt. How about if you say you'll play with me later?

Nick: O.K. Do we have enough ideas? Are we ready to go to step C and choose a solution?

Jackson: Well, I think we need to put some ideas together. How's this? I'll remember to ask to play with you instead of just taking your toys, and you invite me more often.

Nick: I like that. . . Then if I don't want to play, I'll just say I'll play with you later. How about that?

Jackson: Yeah

Nick: Like the songs says, when you ch ch ch ch choose, you leave the b b b b blues. I feel better already!

Peacemaker: Good! Now what's next?

Jackson: Well it seems like we made a deal. . . How about if we shake on it and do step D -- do it.

Nick: Here's my hand.

Jackson: Here's mine.

Peace Table Steps D and E:
Do it and Evaluate Lesson

Goals:
1. To implement a "Do-It" plan
2. To look at the plan after it has been implemented and determine its effectiveness
3. To celebrate an effective conflict resolution plan to build trust and encourage future problem solving behavior

Materials:
1. *Do It Rap* and *Celebrate* song from *We Can Solve it Peacefully* audiotape
2. Two puppets (Sarah and Jamie) with four blocks
3. Popcorn popper and popcorn
4. Conflict Resolution Chart
5. Drum
6. Chart paper from previous lessons and a new, blank one, or *Peacemaker's A,B,Cs of Conflict Resolution*™ (poster)

Presentation:
1. Choose a child to invite children to community with a drum.

2. Children invite *Peacemaker*ᔆᴹ to community.

3. *Peacemaker*ᔆᴹ greets the children and says, "Because you know how to do step A, B and C, you are ready to do the last two steps today. D-Do It and E-Evaluate. Let's make a D paper and an E paper." (Write Do It and Evaluate, or show them on the ready-made chart.)

4. Teacher invites two children to bring puppets Sarah and Jamie to the peace table located in the center of the community.

5. *Peacemaker*ᔆᴹ says, "Before I go today, I would like to share some of my popcorn with you and celebrate the time we have had together. I brought popcorn because popping corn reminds me

of brainstorming. Each time one of the kernels pops, it's like a new idea. Every time we hear or see popcorn popping we'll be able to remember our time togehter when we were learning how to be more peaceful to ourselves and to each other.

5. Today we will do the last two steps, D and E.

6. "Who would like to do the puppet play today showing Sarah's and Jamie's win-win solution for the D step, Do It?" (Choose two volunteers.)

7. "Before our volunteers do the puppet play, I would like to share the *Do It Rap* song with you." (Play the song, or see the next page. Discuss if the children have questions about the words. Review the words with the children.)

8. "O.K., let's begin the puppet play! (Remind the puppeteers of the chosen solution and invite them to act it out.) "Let's clap for our puppeteers." (Thank them for participating and ask them to return to the community.)

9. "E is Evaluate. Evaluate means to decide if the solution or choice solved the problem. If both people think the plan solved their problem they *Celebrate*! Do you think Sarah and Jamie solved their problem?" *Yes!* "Then it's time to celebrate. The pupppets want to give each other a high five first!" (Begin making the popcorn. Play the song and dialog, and turn the tape over for the rest of the songs that follow, while you pass out popcorn and juice to the children.)

10. After the children have their popcorn party, *Peacemaker Puppet*™ says, "Because you know all the steps for using a peace table now, I'm going to give you this peace table! All we need to do is decide on a special place to put it with the Conflict Resolution Chart." (Class decides where to put it.) "Congratulations on all your peacemaking work. I'm going to send a letter home to your moms and dads and tell them how much I enjoyed working with you. Now all of you know how the peace table works and you can teach it to the rest of your family. Maybe you would even like to ask your mom and dad if you can have a peace table at your home. Thank you for letting me show you the peace table. I'm going to ask your teacher to put me in the drama area tomor

row so you can talk to me and play with me anytime you want. I love you!"

Empowerment of the Children:
1. Inviting other children to community
2. Inviting *Peacemaker Puppet*^{TM}
3. Bringing necessary supplies to community
4. Doing a puppet play
5. Deciding the location of the peace table

Points of Interest:
1. Seeing the popcorn popper
2. Watching the popcorn popper have a "brainstorm"
3. Seeing a puppet play being done by peers
4. Celebrating a win-win solution and eating popcorn
5. *Peacemaker Puppet*^{TM} becoming part of the drama area

Extensions and Variations:
1. **Have a face-painting party** and paint peace symbols on children's faces so they look like *Peacemaker.*
2. **Demonstrate some fancy "high-fives"** as another way to celebrate.
3. **Brainstorm other ways to celebrate** that don't cost money.
4. **Teach a new familiar song** (tune of *I'm a Little Teapot*).
I'm a little peacemaker just this size, (hands on head)
My head and my heart are very wise. (hands on head then heart)
When my head looks around and sees a tear, (hands on head, turn side to side, then draw fingers down face under eyes like tears run down)
My heart knows love is needed there! (hands on heart until word "there," then point out).

Do It Rap

Now D is for do it, gonna try our plan,
If it doesn't work out, we'll just try again.
Now everybody chooses a different do it don't they?
Some might choose to hug-a-bug-a-lug-a-rug-a won't they?
Others choose to stop-an-arm-a-swinging-and-a-binging
Some might want to take some time to hear the choir singing
But anyway your thinking, the do it bell's a ringing.

Now D is for do it, gonna try our plan,
Try to do it fairly now -- trust and take a chance.
Now every plan necessitates-a different do it, don't it?
Some might choose to take-a-turn-to-talk-upon-the-phonit
Others choose to care-a-share-a-pair of chocolate donuts
But whether it's a stop-a-turn-a-hug-a-bug- or walka,
Do your plan together now -- walka what you talka.

Language Development:
1. Do It
2. Evaluate
3. Celebrate

Additional Reading Step D:
R. Charlip and B. Supree (1972). "Harlequin and the Gift of Many Colors," *Parents Magazine.* Can be borrowed from the Philadelphia Yearly Meeting Library, 1515 Cherry St. Phila., PA 19102.
J. Charters and M.Foreman (1961), *The General.* Routledge and Kegan (Grades PreK-3).
R. Wezel (1961). *The Good Bird,* Harper (Philadelphia Yearly Meeting Library).
Ryerson. Johnson (1963). *The Monkey and the Wild, Wild Wind,* Abelord, (Phila. Yearly Meeting)
Stanford Summers (1969). *Wacky and His Fiddlejig,* (Phila. Yearly Meeting)
L. Lionni (1969). *The Alphabet Tree,* Harper and Row.
E. Kastner (1949). *The Animals Conference,* David McGay (Phila. Yearly Meeting).
W. Wondriska (1970). *All the Animals Were Angry,* Holt (Grades PreK-3).
M. Careme (1982). *The Peace,* Green Tiger Press (Grades PreK-3).
F. Z. Bradenberg (1977). *Nice New Neighbors,* Scholastic Books, PO Box 7502 Jefferson City, MO (Grades PreK-K).
Additional Reading Step E:
M. Sharrat, *I'm Not Oscar's Friend Anymore* (Grades PreK-1).

E is Evaluate.
If you like your plan
Celebrate

When we solve a problem with our friends or family,
That everybody looked at very differently,
When we solve a problem, the best thing we all do,
Is celebrate, celebrate, celebrate working it through.

Celebrate, working it through.
Celebrate, with your friends and you.
Celebrate, working it through.
Celebrate, celebrate, celebrate, is what we do.

L. Fitzhugh (1965). *Bang, Bang, You're Dead,* Harper and Row (Phila. Yearly Meeting).
R. Kennedy (1979). *The Lost Kingdom Of Karnica,* Sierra Club Books (Grades K-4).
B. Baker (1969). *The Pig War,* Harper and Row (Phila. Yearly Meeting).
C. Pomerantz (1974). *The Princess and the Admiral,* Addison-Wesley.
J. Muller and Jorg Steiner (1983). *The Sea People,* Shocken (Grades 1-4).
N. Babbitt (1969). *The Search for Delicious,* Farrar, Straus and Groux.
M. Foreman (1974). *War and Peas,* Crowell (Grades PreK-3).

Chapter V   The Top of the Pyramid:
Empowerment as a Peacemaker
Great Peacemakers to Inspire
Young Minds

When great peacemakers are invited into the classroom community through literature, videos, and as guests, it provides a tremendous opportunity for children to discover powerful mentors and to find the inspiration they need, in order to continue to be peacemakers even in the face of social and/or personal chaos.

Leaders of the past and the present have given tremendously of their gifts, their time, their commitment, their knowledge and their lives. They inspire us with their abilities to analyze, synthesize and give understandable overviews of complex subjects. They provide leadership to help us be aware of and alleviate oppression. For some of them, providing this leadership means risking their own lives. Their courage helps us to move forward for peace and be leaders when we need to be. Some are highly creative and think of and do alternatives to violence never before imagined. They have added to our peacemaking tool box and inspire us to use our creativity with unsolved problems.

Whatever their backgrounds or their contributions, peacemakers all over the world are extremely fascinating. When we share their lives with our children, peace education becomes an intriguing journey. Acts of violence begin to pale in comparison, and appear simplistic. No longer do we receive their seductive and addictive powers in ignorance. Their appeal is more apt to fade as our awareness of great peacemakers grows.

After hearing a story of a great peacemaker, invite the children to formulate questions they would like to know about that person. Let their questions guide you.

The children have great capacity to be peacemakers, and can be a constant source of inspiration for us as well.

Resources:

Armed With Courage. May McNeer and Lynda Ward. Abingdon Press, Nashville, TN. 1957. Short stories about seven people who spent their lives working for peace and justice. Biographies include: Florence Nightingale, Father Damien, George Washington Carver, Jane Addams, Wilfred Grenfell, Mahatma Gandhi and Albert Schweitzer.

Big Red. (Video) Scholastic, Inc., PO Box 7502, Jefferson City, MO 65102. Grades PreK-2. A real-life children's adventure into the exciting world of everyday heroes; the brave people and mighty equipment that fight fires. (25 minutes)

Don't Ride the Bus on Monday. Prentice-Hall, Englewood Cliffs, NJ. 1973. Rosa Parks' courage and conviction is evident in the story of her refusal to give up her seat on the bus. Her nonviolent protest sparked a campaign to end discrimination in the United States.

Francis, the Poor Man of Assisi. Tomie DePaola. 1982. Holiday House, New York, NY. Written to celebrate the eight hundredth anniversary of St. Francis of Assisi, the book tells the story of a man who exchanged a life of wealth and luxury to serve the poor and needy for the cause of peace.

Gladdys Makes Peace. Jan Hogan. 1985. Brethren Press, 1451 Dundee Ave., New York, NY 60120. Grades PreK-2. A picture book biography of the outstanding peace educator, Gladdys Ester Muir (Can Be Borrowed from Phila. Yearly Meeting, 92 Mui J)

Manual for the PeaceMaker: An Iroquois Legend to Heal Self and Society, Jean Houston. 1995. Quest Books, Wheaton, IL A book for adults which invites you to participate in a legend about a bringer of peace, a creator of community, a changer of his world.

Peace Be With You. Cornelia Lehn. Faith and Life, 1981. Grades PreK-6. Fifty-nine stories of men and women who have believed in the way of peace and lived accordingly. Good for reading aloud in groups which span generations. The list of acknowledgments at the end which gives the source of each story is a treasure in itself.

Picture Book Biographies. World Almanac Education (PO Box 94556, Cleveland, OH 44101). Grades PreK-2. Easy-to-read biographies are an excellent resource for early grades. Facts and personality are expertly mixed. Choices available: Thomas Jefferson, Helen Keller, Abraham Lincoln, Eleanor Roosevelt, George Washington, Simon Bolivar, Frederick Douglas, Anne Frank, John Kennedy, Florence Nightingale, Jesse Owens, Harriet Tubman, Rosa Parks, and Sitting Bull.

A Picture Book of Martin Luther King, Jr. (video) Kimbo Educational, P.O. Box 477, Dept. V, Long Branch, NJ 07740. Grades PreK-4. A thoughtful and thorough recounting of the events of Dr. King's times, the major turning point in his life, and his accomplishments as a civil leader.

The Picture Life Of Martin Luther King. 1968. Margaret B. Young. Franklin Watts Inc., 730 Fifth Ave., New York, NY 10019. (Can be borrowed from Ohil. Yearly Meeting 325ZBK) Grades PreK-3. Brief and simple text with large pictures tells the story of King's life and stresses his message of love-power.

The Picture Life of Ralph J. Bunche. Margaret B. Young. 1968. Franklin Watts Inc., 730 Fifth Ave., New York, NY 10019. (Can be borrowed from Phila. Yearly Meeting, 325.2B BJ) Grades PreK-3. Simple text and many pictures bring to life this story of a man whose work with the U.N. was to help make peace.

Quanah Parker: Indian Warrior for Peace. LaVere Anderson. 1970. Garrard Publishing Co., Champaign, IL. Grades 2-5. A true account, based on the life of an Indian warrior who had a Native American father and a European American mother. Contains the message that all people in a nation must unite for peace.

Rosa Parks. Eloise Greenfield. 1973. Crowell, Grades 2-4. This biography focuses on Rosa Parks' 1955 resistance to segregation on the busses of Montgomery, Alabama, and to the boycott and subsequent Supreme Court order which required the bus company to change its rules.

The Story of William Penn. 1964. Aliki. Prentice-Hall, Grades 2-4. William Penn's biography shows how adhering to one's peaceful beliefs despite persecution pays off in the end. It enabled Penn to befriend the Native Americans, and to develop a trusting community based on fairness.

Ted Studebaker: A Man Who Loved Peace. Joy Hofacker Moore. 1987. Herald Press, Scottdale, PA. Story of Ted Studebaker and how he spent his life working for peace.

20th Century American Heroes. Shirley Cook. The Learning Shop, Highland Gates Center, 706 S. Gammon Rd., Madison, WI 53719 or call (608) 277-8747. Grades K-3. Students will develop higher-level thinking skills in all areas of the curriculum as they participate in activities that teach and inspire. Selected heroes: Martin Luther King, Jr., Amelia Earhart, Walt Disney, Dr. Seuss, and Helen Keller.

Reverence For Life: The Words of Albert Schweitzer. Harold E. Robles. Grades: PreK-6. (Needs to be adapted for younger children.) In one collection for the first time, here are inspiring words by Albert Schweitzer -- winner of the 1952 Nobel Peace Prize. These excerpt from previously unpublished letters illustrate his "reverence for life" -- respect for the lives of all beings and a demand for the highest development of an individual's resources. The thread of this inspirational belief appears throughout these deeply insightful writings and shows Schweitzer's commitment to creating global consciousness and cultivating dignity toward all people.

Samantha Smith: Journey to the Soviet Union. Samantha Smith. 1985. Little Brown and Co., 34 Beacon St., Boston, MA 02106. Grades 2-6. Samantha Smith was the schoolgirl who asked, "Why do the Russians want to blow us up?" and then invited to visit the Soviet Union. This book, 122 pages, is filled with photographs and memories of her visit.

The Story of Johnny Appleseed. Aliki. 1963. Prentice-Hall, Inc., Cliffs, NJ. Grades PreK-2. Johnny Chapman never carried a gun although he traveled alone in a country filled with wild animals and with Native Americans whom most European settlers thought were dangerous. Johnny's gentle manner befriended animals, settlers, and Indians. Appleseed spread a message of peace wherever he went as he traveled around with a bag full of apple seeds on his back and a cooking pan on his head. Johnny's story serves to remind children to spread peace in many ways. (92 CJ)

Young Children Rap. Chris Meissel. The Learning Shop, Highland Gates Center, 706 S. Gammon Rd., Madison, WI 53719 or call (608) 277-8747. Grades PreK. An engaging collection of raps, rhymes, and learning activities that reinforce basic skills as they introduce preschoo-age children to notable African-Americans.

The Philadelphia Yearly Meeting Library, 1515 Cherry St. Philadelphia, PA 19102, has many of these books. Write for instructions on how to borrow from the library.

Social Action and Service Projects for
Empowering Young Peacemakers

When we have lived in peaceful classroom communities and experienced implicit and explicit peace education, we become *capable* of living peaceful lives. Children desire to take their peacemaking skills to the larger society and help create more peaceful communities through service and social action. With our skills, and the continual inspiration of famous historical peacemakers and current peacemakers, we are prepared to begin assessing the needs within our own communities and to discover opportunities to make a difference. When children are involved with social action and service projects at a young age, they develop a long and rich history of being involved in issues which affect their lives.

When we don't include children in the process of deciding how we are going to live our lives together, we teach and model oppression. They learn, "People who are bigger use power over people who are smaller and weaker." Thus, rather than focusing on community, some children spend an enormous amount of time trying to figure out how they are going to get some of that power through violence and oppressing others. It is the authors' belief that we will begin to solve many other forms of oppression when we all learn to respect and preserve the rights of children.

Children have the right to grow up in peaceful classrooms and peaceful homes. They also have the right to learn peacemaking skills as young children. Why is this important? Peacemaking skills are not learned overnight. They are learned as a *process* much like math, science, and history. For example: we don't expect young children to be able to do statistical analysis, but we do ask them to study and practice math skills at a very early age. To participate in solving community problems is a developmental process as well. When we invite children to partici-pate, the surprise we often find is the children's stunning capability and capacity for seeing and practicing peace in ways that we can learn from.

If we take the time to reflect back to our own child-hood with the question, "What was happening in the world, my country, community or my neighborhood that I was seriously concerned, worried or scared about?" we begin to realize that *the desire for social action appears early in life*. As children, we wanted something to be done about war, poverty and violence, and so on, and many of us were eager and willing to work on these issues but were not empowered to do so. Instead, what happened to so many us, and continues to this day, is that our parents tried to alleviate our fears, concern or distress over these issues. They were well-meaning, perhaps they believed, "You are a child only once and I want you to enjoy your childhood. There will be plenty of time later to deal with these matters. Go and play." or "You are so young and the problems are so complex. You have to wait until you are older to do something about this. Study hard and maybe someday you will have a contribution to make." Worse yet, maybe you had a great idea for a social problem but nobody would even listen to you because you were a child.

Dream and Do, Dreams Come True
by Julie P. Peterson and Rebecca A. Janke

Whatever we've done once began as a thought;
Some have been violent, what have we wrought?
Surrounded by pain, murder, war, and dismay,
We've all played a part in our way.

(Chorus) Dream and do, dreams come true.

We've had peace heros who walked in the light
And we must continue their nonviolent fight
Without hatred or guns, their visions held true,
And we need new heros like you.

You have the power to make a new way,
Take the hand of the partners you meet on your way.
The visions of peace that you hold in your mind,
Can be real for all humankind.

When we begin to create an environment for social action, it's important to dialog with children. Listen to their stories. Listen for their concerns. True empowerment for the children comes from realizing that their experiences, shared with others' experiences, are a catalyst for action. The following six step process will encourage the dialog to begin, and will result in social action which is pertinent to the children's lives.

1. **The first step** is children telling stories about their lives which describe their concerns about the world, nation, or neighborhood. After telling the story, children are asked if there is anything he/she thinks should be changed or stopped in order for the situation to be fair or more peaceful. Very young children can be jump started for these kinds of discussions, if they are not forthcoming, by asking, "If you were the boss of the world, or the boss of the school or the boss of the playground, what do you think should be done about _____?"

To be able to say before others, "I would like _____to stop," or "I think _____should be changed helps children to move beyond *internalized oppression* ("This is just the way life is." or "Somehow I must deserve this." "There is nothing that can be done.")

After stories are gathered over a period of a few days or a few weeks, the group can decide by consensus, what social action project they would like to work on together. It's important that the children work together in a collective body rather, than having groups with different projects in the same community. To stay in community and accomplish a task in community will give the group more power, tasks can be spread out so to avoid being overwhelmed, and the experience of solidarity empowers children to see the benefits of organizing themselves as a group over an important issue.

If the children are unable to determine a social action project from the story gathering, our job becomes one of increasing the children's awareness of existing social problems and asking the children what they think about certain issues and what they would like to see done about them. Exposing the children to peacemakers who are working for change, and the stories of people who are experiencing injustice, will touch their hearts and inspire all of us to work for change.

Regardless of which avenue is chosen to determine the social action project, children begin to believe that their opinions and ideas matter, and are highly valued. This is critical to their self-esteem. The children hear, "We matter and I matter."

2. **The second step** provides an opportunity to brainstorm ideas that might solve or begin to solve the social problem the community has chosen.

3. **In the third step** the community decides which ideas look "doable." Discussion centers around resources available such as time, energy, money, supplies, and so on.

4. **The fourth step** involves exploring strategies to make the "doables" happen. Asking ourselves some questions like: How are we going to raise our money? Maybe we could do this without money if we _____. What do we need to find out before we can do _____? Who can help us with _____?

5. **The next step** is developing the action plan. What can we do in the next week to move toward our goals? Everyone in the group volunteers for one or more tasks. *Birthlines*, rather than deadlines, are established. People's names are written down with his/her tasks so everyone knows who is doing what. The next planning meeting date is established to determine the action for another week.

6. **The sixth step** is implementing the action plan. Step 5 and 6 work hand-in-hand, since some of the action plan will be in development while other parts of it will be completed.

In using these few steps, the teacher's role is to help the children facilitate their own work. It's important to remember to use humor or silliness along the journey. Even though the work is serious, we want to celebrate with laughter and share the joys of community. In this way we are peaceful to ourselves as we try to bring more peace to the world.

We also will be carrying wonderful memories as we move on with our lives and find ourselves in other communities. These memories will give us strength to begin working for peace again in new environments or to create a desire in our children to pass these memories along to their children.

Research from the National Youth Leadership Council shows that when you integrate service or social action opportunities into classroom instruction it has other benefits:
1. Enhancing academic performance and engagement for <u>all</u> youth
2. Developing critical thinking skills
3. Promoting a caring school climate
4. Improving self-esteem and self-concept
5. Reinforcing moral development
6. Building attitudes and skills for active citizenship
7. Promoting a view of youth (and self) as valued resources
8. Enhancing motivation for continued peacemaking.

One of the joys of doing social action with children is seeing how quickly they tap into their empathy and compassion. Projects are seldom done because it is the "right thing to do." They are done because the children "feel a need to show their love." Children have just as much need to give love as to receive love.

Piaget believed that children could not express empathy until the age of eight. However, those of us who have worked in the field, know this not the case. For example, Laura Reed, author of "Amos Bear Gets Hurt," (*Young Children*, May 1995) shares a delightful research project on empathy: She bandaged the center's large stuffed teddy bear on his arm. When the children arrived in the morning, their response in caring for Amos was intense. Each child had an immediate idea of how best to care for the bear. They immediately went into problem solving with a great deal of give-and-take. Throughout the morning they treated him with the utmost care and tenderness. He was cradled in someone's arms all morning. He was not allowed to bump into things and was passed from hand to hand with great delicacy.

All of us have stories we can share of young children reaching out to others with loving behaviors. *Creating empathy is not the task before us. Creating opportunities with children to share their great capacity for love, is our task.*

Organizations and Opportunities:

About World Hunger, Church World Service, PO Box 968, Elkhart, IN 46515-0968. A fifteen page booklet containing information on hunger, myths associated with the issue, causes and actions that can be taken to produce short and long term solutions.

Acid Rain Foundation, 1410 Varsity Drive, Raleigh, NC 27606. (919) 828-9443. Education materials for K-12.

Adopt A Stream Foundation, PO Box 5558, Everett, WA 98201. Guidelines for adopting a stream or wetland. Send a SASE and a small donation, if possible.

American Oceans Campaign, 725 Arizona Ave., Suite 102, Santa Monica, CA 90401. (213) 452-2206. Information on protecting the ocean habitat.

American Society For The Prevention Of Cruelty To Animals (ASPCA), Education Department, 441 East 92nd Street, New York, NY 10128. (212) 876-7700. Educational materials on humane treatment of animals.

Econet, 3228 Sacramento Street, San Francisco, CA 94115. (415) 923-0900. International computer-based communication system for environmental preservation.

International Children's Disarmament Day. Atrium Society Publications. International Children's Disarmament Day is a day of fun dedicated to a serious purpose: helping young people reflect on the role of war toys and aggressive play in their lives. Atrium encourages like-minded individuals, schools, and peace groups to sponsor a local Children's Disarmament Day. For full information, please contact Jane Duchesneau at 1-800-848-6021.

International Day Of Peace. United Nations. The third Tuesday of September was declared by the United Nations General Assembly in November 1981 to be a date "officially dedicated and observed as the International Day of Peace and shall be devoted to commemorating and strengthening the ideals of peace both within and among all nations and peoples." (Resolution 36/67) At 10:00 AM on that day the Peace Bell in front of the UN is rung, followed by a moment of silence. Do whatever you can to encourage the annual observance of the Day of Peace in your community, state, and nation.

Kids For Saving The Earth Club. (Newsletter) PO Box 47247, Plymouth, MN 55447. Clinton Hill was only 11 when he died of cancer, but his dream of a cleaner, healthier planet lives on through KSE. This newsletter is packed full of specific ways in which children can help our planet survive.

Ideas:

Toy Giveaway. Talk about the "give away" principle which comes from the Native American tradition and then invite the children to give away one toy of their own to needy children within the community.

Raise funds for children in need. A new playground was built for children with AIDS and HIV positive children with funds raised by children in Ft. Lauderdale, Florida. Help meet a need in your own community through a fundraising project. The Umbrella Project Inc., in New York sells umbrellas designed by children to benefit ill children, particularly those with AIDS. For more information, call 212-794-2934.

Start a peaceful families bookshelf. Collect nonviolent, family-oriented books, videos, and games. Lend them to families in the community. Include books on noted peacemakers. Compile and make copies of a list of cooperative activities that families can do together. Alternative's Book List has many terrific resources. Call (404) 961-0102 for a catalog.

Establish a peace house or sanctuary. Jim Offult, A Mennonite pastor near Chicago, proposes establishing "peace houses." These facilities could become neutral zones where young people could work at peaceful conflict resolution in crisis situations. Or they could simply serve as drop-in centers for children and youths, offering supervised recreation or study.

Save endangered wildflowers of your region. Write: National Wildflower Research Center: 2600 FM 973 North, Austin, TX 78725 or call (512) 929-3600.

Create a backyard habitat. Habitat is important for the survival of animals. Write to Kids For Saving the Earth, P.O. Box 47247, Plymouth, MN 55447-0247 for information on how to get started.

If you buy something that comes in a container that is nonrecyclable, send it back with a letter asking the people who make it to switch to Earth-positive packaging.

Protect forests in North America. The forests are called, "Kids For Saving Earth Children's Forests." This means you can buy and protects acres of forest in North America, just like you can buy and protect acres of rain forest on other continents. Write to Kids For Saving the Earth, P.O. Box 47247, Plymouth, MN 55447-0247 for more details.

Grow George Washington's Trees. Even though we've heard about George Washington cutting down the cherry tree, he was a tree lover. He planted acres of sycamore trees and some of them are still living today, two centuries later. Kids for Saving Earth and the Global ReLeaf program of The American Forestry Association are making it possible for you to plant trees that have very interesting histories. You can get permission to plant them in lots of different places. How about a George Washington grove at your neighborhood park? Maybe seedlings from seeds that visited the moon could be planted around your setting. And what about a Martin Luther King Jr. grove at your school? Dr. King gave speeches about peace and justice under trees. Maybe you can too. For more information about how you can participate, write to KSE/Global ReLeaf - Famous and Historic Trees Project, Kids for Saving Earth, P.O. Box 47247, Plymouth, MN 55447.

Establish a relationship with a sister school. Draw pictures and send dictated stories about peace and desire for peace in the world. (Include pictures of yourselves and the place you live). Help raise money and send any necessary supplies they request.

Shopping Bag Diplomacy. Make a tote bag or school bag with the message, WAR IS NOT HEALTHY FOR CHILDREN AND OTHER LIVING THINGS. Take your bag with you when you go shopping to spread the message. Buy your own fabric and get the stencil for this message from Janet K. Smith, 555 Chippewa Tr., Carol Stream, IL 60188.

Do an act of kindness.

Start a Random Acts of Kindness Club.

Say a peaceful word.

Clean up trash in the neighborhood.

Don't ask for war toys for presents. Turn in any war toys you have to a store that will take them. Ask for toys that teach cooperation and caring, like puzzles, blocks, construction sets, coloring books, puppets, musical instruments, tapes, books, kites, and cooperative games.

Provide canned food, blankets, and clothing of all sizes, new or gently used, for adults and children, especially small children to: Yankton Reservation, c/o Charlie Two Bears, PO Box 384, Avon, SD 57315.

Groups who want to give service can make no greater contribution than to help the single parent.
Dr. Patch Adams

Additional Reading

Animal Tracks. Susan Morrison. (PO Box 146, Eureka Springs, AK 72632.) This nonprofit, action-oriented group's mission is to bring individuals, families, communities, businesses and government together to make a real, positive and measurable difference for our environment, and therefore the lives of us all. "Follow the animals. We're off our path through time and we must find our way back. Follow the animals. They know the way. The answers are in their tracks," says Susan Morrison. Through studying animal strategies she shows how we can use those same strategies for saving the environment.

The Big Parade. Ida Mockren. 1982. Honeycomb Press, Grades PreK-K. Ricky marches in a big peace demonstration.

The Call of Service: A Witness To Idealism. Robert Coles.1993. Houghton Mifflin. (Adults) A passionate book that offers timely insight into a deeply human impulse. At a moment when community involvement has once again become part of the national agenda, Coles shed light on the individual urge toward idealistic action -- what inspires and sustains it, how it is expressed, and why it's so necessary to each of us and to society.

Caring: Activities To Teach The Young To Care For Others. Thomas D. Yawkey and Kenneth C. Jones. 1982. Prentice-Hall. Grades PreK-3. This is a guide for parents and teachers to help young children develop a sense of altruism. It includes a 10-page bibliography.

Service is essential to healing and world Peace.
Dr. Patch Adams

Children In Danger: Coping With The Consequences Of Community Violence. James Barabino. Jossey Bass Publishers. This book looks at the way children's lives are affected by violence, comparing the behaviors of children in Lebanon and Mozambique to those in South Central Los Angeles and Chicago. It offers many suggestions for community involvement in strengthening education.

Children First. Penelope Leach. Knopf. 1994. Church World Service, PO Box 968, Elkhart, IN 46515-0968. After spending millions and employing miracle science to help children come into the world, our society paradoxically denies economic and social supports for children during their crucial years of development. Leach presents specific steps for what we as individuals and a society must do to fashion a new economic priority for all children.

Educating For Peace And Justice: Global Dimensions. James and Kathleen McGinnis. 1984. Institute for Peace and Justice, 4144 Lindell Blvd., St. Louis, MN 63110. Grades 3-6. Resource for teachers on hunger, foreign policy, military, war, global poverty, and other topics plus resource sections.

Evans Corner. Elizabeth Hill. 1967. Holt, Rinehart and Winston, New York, NY. Story of a small boy who discovers that a peacemaker cannot stay within his own room, but must help others in the world as well.

Experiencing More With Less. Meredith Sommers Dregni. 1983. Herald Press (Can be borrowed from Phila. Yearly Meeting Library 301.42Dre) Grades PreK-6. Exciting intergenerational curriculum to help groups learn about responsible living. Creatively and faithfully captures and encapsulates the meaning of the five standards of Don Jansen Longacre's "Living More With Less".

For Every Child, A Better World. Kermit the Frog, as told to Louise Gikow and Ellen Weiss. 1993. United Nations. Grades PreK-3. Brian Henson, the son of Jim Henson, creator of the Muppets, writes: "It was my father's dream to make the world a better place for children everywhere. This book is one of the ways we are keeping this dream alive. We believe this book can help children become the kind of adults who will make the world a better place." This book is inspired by the United Nations Convention on the Rights of the Child. "Every child needs food to eat, but sometimes there isn't enough to go around." The illustrations contrast well-fed muppet characters sitting at a full table, with bony-framed muppets holding empty bowls, and wearing sad expressions on their faces. A palatable way for young children to learn about the inequities in our world, and begin to understand how important it is to work for justice. A listing of organizations working to ensure better living conditions for all children and adults is given at the end of the book.

The Generator: National Journal Of Service-Learning And Youth Leadership. Editor: Madeleine Wegner. National Youth Leadership Council. The primary benefit of NYLC membership (Call 612-631-3672 for details). Semiannual publication written by service-learning practitioners and devoted to covering the latest project ideas, curricula, policy decisions and research in the field. Through Service-Learning Training Institutes, The National Youth Leadership Council offers local, regional and national staff development to educators, youth professionals, and all those interested in youth service. One, two, and three day Training Institutes are tailored to meet the specific needs of your students, schools and regions.

Guerillas Of Goodness Handbook. Molli Nickell. 1994. Workman Publishing. All ages. Here are 127 inspiring ways for all ages to make a big difference in the world. Charming illustrations in a pocket-sized book depict simple yet thoughtful acts of goodness that help improve others' lives.

The Happy Prince. Oscar Wilde. 1965. Prentice-Hall.(Can be borrowed from Phila. Yearly Meeting Library, 2301 JFW.) Grades 1-6. The Prince is beautiful but unhappy; with the help of a sparrow he learns that the only precious things are good deeds.

Helping. James Levin. Scholastic, Inc. Grades PreK-2 Delightful photos and rhyming verse show children the joys of helping others.

Helping Hands Handbook. Patricia Adams and Jean Marxollo. 1993. Random House. Grades 2-6. For kids 8 and up who want to help people, animals and the world we live in. Includes practical ideas and upbeat, real stories from kids who have made significant contributions to their communities and the lives of others.

Hunger On Spaceship Earth. Resource Packet. American Friends Service Committee, 15 Rutherford Place, New York, NY 10003. An action-oriented resource packet including background readings, classroom exercises and questionnaires, alternative non-meat diets, resources, a simulation game, wall charts, and action suggestions.

In The Tiger's Mouth: An Empowerment Guide For Social Action, Katrina Shields. 1993. New Society Publishers, 4527 Springfield Ave., Phila., PA 19143.(Adult) A wealth of practical ideas and approaches for curing the stress and burnout experienced by people dedicated to healing our society and earth. Provides exercises and successful examples for building sustainable organizations, groups and activist lives.

Kids' Random Acts Of Kindness. Conari Press. 1994. Grades PreK-6. Kids share their stories about random acts of kindness in which they participated, or of which they were the recipients. Write for a free easy to use, inspirational guide for educators on how to teach a unit on RAOK in the classroom. It includes the latest research on the physiological and psychological effects of doing good, a list of suggested activities, and information on how to get involved with other participating schools across the country. Write to Conari Press for a teacher's guide.

Learning By Giving: K-8 Service-Learning Curriculum Guide, Rich Willits Cairn with Theresa Cable. National Youth Leadership Council. Grades K-8. Structured as a student-driven framework for developing curriculum-based service-learning activities. Includes an overview of service-learning basics and initiative games. Through environmental, intergenerational and multicultural service activities, identifies potential personal and academic outcomes.

Make A World Of Difference. Roots and Wings Catalog. Grades PreK-6. A fabulous handbook loaded with creative learning activities to teach about global interdependence and international development issues. Activities for all ages on hunger, peace, community building, cooking, drama, crafts, event organization.

Our Town: A Simulation Of Contemporary Community Issues. Katherine Ruggieri-Vande Putte. Zephyr Press, 3316 N Chapel Ave., PO Box 66006-B, Tucson, AZ 85728. Grades 2-6. Get students involved with an interactive simulation that teaches community cooperation skills. Bring local community issues into your classroom with role-playing activities. Give students the opportunity to earn a living, buy groceries and hardware supplies, use a bank, and make decisions involving their homes and personal finances. Help your students experience how the community impacts the individual and how they must work together to make decisions about community issues.

The Peace Book, Bernard Benson. Bantam Books, Toronto, Canada. 1982. The story of a little boy who declares "I want to live," and sets out on a mission to expose the dangers of nuclear warheads. He meets with world leaders, united children as well as adults and devises an exchange program which brings peace to the world.

The Peaceful Classroom: 162 Easy Activities to Teach Preschoolers Compassion and Cooperation, (1993). Charles Smith, Gryphon House, 3706 Otis St. Mt. Rainer MD 20712

Peace Porridge One: Kids As Peacemakers. Teddy Milne. Pittenbruach Press, Northampton, MA. 1987. Grades K-6. 291 pages filled with activities to help children catch the excitement of working for peace. Major sections include First Steps, Things to Do, Thoughts and Projects, and Resources and Groups.

Perspectives: A Teaching Guide To Concepts Of Peace. Educators for Social Responsibility. 1983. (Can be borrowed from Phila.Yearly Meeting, 341.1Edu) Grades K-6. An extensive and well-organized guide designed to help students consider choices and alternatives for the future and to feel involved in creating that future. Students are encouraged to analyze peace, to understand it as a positive, active stance, and to examine the ways peace can be promoted and preserved. Examines obstacles to peace such as propaganda and the "enemy" and takes a look at peacemakers and workers for social change.

*Something Magical. (*Can be borrowed from the Philadelphia Yearly Meeting Library. VHS 30 min.) In a unique approach to the process of learning concern and care for others, this video highlights a triumph over prejudice toward the handicapped with a touching story of personal and group achievement. Teresa Maebori, a third-and-fourth-grade teacher at Germantown Friends School in Philadelphia, was upset when her students performed a skit that mimicked the physically and mentally handicapped. Maebori resolved to give her students an opportunity to experience a greater understanding of such persons. She initiated a class project which involved pairing up her students with children aged 4 to 16 who were students at a school for children with cerebral palsy. The students joined together in a six-month project to put on a musical play entitled, "The Other Side of the Fence." The film captures a very special event and the invaluable bonds that developed between the students. Bronze Apple, 1991 National Education Film and Video Festival; Gold Award, 1990 John Muir Medical Film Festival. Rental $10.00 for two days.